PALMISTRY: YOUR CAREER IN YOUR HANDS

PALMISTRY: YOUR CAREER IN YOUR HANDS

HOW HAND ANALYSIS CAN BRING SUCCESS & SELF-FULFILMENT

NATHANIEL ALTMAN & ANDREW FITZHERBERT

Illustrated by Linda James

THE AQUARIAN PRESS

First published as *Career, Success and Self-Fulfilment* 1988
This edition 1989

© NATHANIEL ALTMAN and ANDREW FITZHERBERT 1988

British Library Cataloguing in Publication Data

Altman, Nathaniel
[Career, success and self-fulfilment]. Palmistry:
your career in your hands.
1. Palmistry
I. [Career, success and self-fulfilment].   II. Title
III. Fitzherbert, Andrew
133.6

ISBN 0-85030-884-4

*The Aquarian Press is part of the Thorsons Publishing Group,
Wellingborough, Northamptonshire, NN8 2RQ, England*

Printed in Great Britain by Woolnough Bookbinding Limited,
Irthlingborough, Northamptonshire

1   3   5   7   9   10   8   6   4   2

CONTENTS

PART I:
PALMISTRY: THE ESSENTIALS

Chapter 1

CAREERS FOR A FUTURE: NEW DIRECTIONS, NEW HORIZONS

Since the widespread introduction and utilization of computers during the 1960s, the job scene has changed dramatically. As we continue to move further into the 'age of information' and away from the industrial age, our relationship to work – and the kinds of tasks we perform – will continue to change rapidly.

The traditional pursuit of a secure job, fixed life goals, career specialization, and the drive to be a 'success' has been challenged by the fast moving and often revolutionary technological developments taking place in both the developed and Third World nations. Jobs which once seemed absolutely secure have now disappeared, while certain modern job descriptions – especially in the field of computers and telecommunications – would have been totally unrecognizable twenty years ago.

For those who desire to expand their career possibilities, these rapid changes have helped bring about creative new strategies for the increased utilization of our individual talents, as well as the need for greater personal fulfilment in our careers.

When planning a career, our goals are tending to become more flexible and tentative as opposed to fixed. People are recognizing the need to develop a broad range of skills so that one can perform a variety of tasks within a given family, or families, of jobs rather than excel in one particular type of work.

In addition to specializing in one area of expertise, the trend is to become both a specialist *and* a generalist. Rather than merely being what we would traditionally call 'successful', there is a move towards demanding greater job satisfaction and choosing the kind of work which nourishes the whole person, as opposed to just the ego or the bank balance. As we move closer to the twenty-first century, the opportunities for work that is both financially rewarding and personally fulfilling have perhaps never been greater. At the same time, there is a corresponding need for greater self-understanding and the need to seek out (or create) careers in which we can fully express our personal interests, aptitudes and goals.

TOWARDS A NEW MEANING OF WORK

For many, work consists of merely earning a living. However, when we consider the issues surrounding work and the workplace in more depth, we will find that our jobs involve a major social arena in which a variety of basic human needs are met. Because we are dealing primarily with the psychological aspects of palmistry as they relate to career choice and self-fulfilment, it is important to keep these psychological aspects of work in mind as we proceed through the book, even though at first glance they may not appear to apply to our own personal case.

In addition to earning an income, there is much social status attached to work in our society. Work is viewed as a sign of adulthood and a symbol of independence and self-respect. Even though individuals in their twenties or thirties may have a sufficient income, they often feel the pressure to be gainfully employed. Many people seek work as a result, even though there are other areas into which they could channel their talent and energy. Ironically, there is also pressure (which in some countries is under sanction of law) for people to cease working at a given age even though they may be competent, healthy and eager to continue at their jobs. We will explore the issue of retirement or redundancy in the light of palmistry more fully later on.

On the most fundamental level, work simply provides many people who would ordinarily be drinking at a pub or watching television, with something to do each day. Work creates a structure to their lives, and generates the feeling of being a productive member of society. A crisis may occur when such people (especially men) are laid off or retired. In addition to the previously mentioned problem of loss of status and self-respect, these people have specialized in their work to such an extent that they have not developed (or perhaps even thought of) other, very often complementary, talents and abilities which could utilize their free time. They simply did not consider that there are other areas in which they can devote their energy, talents and interests outside the traditional work environment.

Another important aspect of working is that it enables us to do something for others. Whether or not we do this in an obvious way, like a fireman, a teacher or a physiotherapist, many people appear to need to see their work as purposeful. For the most part, they are angry and frustrated when denied the opportunity to utilize their talents on the job. They often need an activity which links them to goals and purposes which transcend their own.

Finally, it is important to remember that human beings are highly social animals, and work is a primary social activity. In addition to being a place to meet others, the working environment is a stage on which we share experiences outside the nuclear family. How we relate to others at work is a basic indicator of our ability to relate to others in general. For many, the arena of work is where we face many of the personal traumas and challenges which are essential to our growth as human beings. It is also the place where many experience their greatest feelings of success and personal satisfaction. Because these events are often shared with colleagues and co-workers, emotional bonds can be very intense.

For this reason, this book has not been written merely to enable the reader to find the 'perfect career'. Although moving in a career direction which is right for us is of primary importance, we will be dealing with other issues as well. Through a deep understanding of ourselves gained through the study of the hand, we will be able to better understand how we relate to others, how we can adjust to career changes, and discover additional areas we can devote ourselves to, which may be out of the traditional work-for-money environment. By more fully understanding our motivations, needs, talents, difficulties and personal aspirations, we can become more fulfilled and dynamic human beings.

HIDDEN FACTORS BEHIND CAREER CHOICE

In our study of palmistry, career and self-fulfilment, there are several factors which lead us towards a career direction that are of particular interest. The more obvious reasons, such as aptitude and interest in a specific career, will be dealt with in detail in the following chapters. However, the more subtle influences in our career choices can in some cases be as important as the obvious ones.

Not surprisingly, a major influence comes from our parents. Whether the influence is conscious or not, our parents' desire to see us in a particular professional field can be a major one. On the most obvious and fundamental level, parental influence is often based on the child's gender. Girls are introduced from a very early age to typical 'female' activities such as cooking, cleaning and taking care of dolls, which often leads them to a career as a housewife, primary school teacher, secretary, or similar type of 'nurturing' job later on. By the same token, little boys are encouraged to become involved in 'masculine' activities that involve courage, adventure, and the development of manual skills, such as building model cars and aeroplanes.

This type of early parental conditioning often prepares them for further training for jobs as executives, policemen, car mechanics and factory workers. Although this situation is changing somewhat, some people are still astonished when they meet a female fireman, barrister, or managing director of a large company, while male nurses, secretaries and house-husbands continue to be the subjects of conversation.

In some cases, parental pressure takes the form of wanting to extend the family dynasty by producing several generations of doctors, stockbrokers or home-makers. Others may want their children to enter a career which would bring a measure of prestige to an otherwise undistinguished family history. Whether through subtle encouragement or blatant manipulation, the influence of parental pressure in determining the career direction from childhood is worthy of close examination. Very often these emotional 'contracts' we make with our parents lead us into professions for which we are totally unsuited, and which are a source of stress and dissatisfaction throughout our working years.

By the same token, career choice can involve a subtle reaction against parental pressure. Very often we abandon early areas of interest or aptitude which we shared with one or both parents in order to declare our independence or simply to rebel. Some of these early aptitudes and interests could have provided the seeds for a satisfying career. For this reason, career counsellors suggest that we become aware of the unconscious decisions we made years ago so that we can again respond to primary interests and feelings. This exciting process of rediscovery may lead us towards expressing these qualities in our present career, or even to seek retraining for a new or additional line of work.

THE LIFE CYCLE OF WORK

There are other barriers to a fulfilling career. Like the early 'parental tapes' which continue to influence us during childhood, we often harbour feelings of worthlessness and lack of self-esteem. All too often, the hand will reveal an abundance of talent, skills and interests, while a poor self-image – which can also be detected on the hand – undermines the ability to manifest them in the world.

As the ever-changing blueprint of our life, the hand can also reveal the tendency to overestimate our abilities, currents which can lead to technical incompetence, lack of focus, worry, and inability to relate well to others. Due to the fact that problems in these areas are bound to have an impact on both the direction of our career and the level of satisfaction we achieve in our working life, they will be dealt with in more detail in further chapters.

It is also important to place work in its proper perspective. For many people, their jobs tend to compensate for a poor social life, and can be used as an escape from boredom, a difficult relationship, or another problem. When work is used to compensate for feelings of loneliness or despair, it will not create a feeling of personal well-being or satisfaction in the long run.

Age also has much to do with professional well-being. Every seven to ten years we go through important life cycles which reflect different personal and professional needs. While they vary according to each individual, some basic life cycles are as follows:

Early years (20–30)   A time for opportunities and exploration.

Building years (30–40)   A time for solidifying our career choice. This is often a period of dynamic changes in the form of traumas, problems and challenges.

Transitional years (40–50)   A period of reduced economic pressure, with new opportunities for enjoyment and an increased desire for personal growth.

Mature years (50–60)   Often seen as years of lowered enthusiasm and decline, this period can also be a time for new discoveries and professional redirection.

Golden years (60 and beyond)   Usually considered a period of relaxation, retirement, loneliness and boredom, it can also be considered a time for utilizing experience and accumulated wisdom in new areas of creativity, leisure and service.

These cycles show that life involves continuous changes. We need to manage these changes and adapt to our present needs, in order to get the most out of our particular situation. As mentioned earlier, our career should be more than just a job, or an activity which only contributes to our basic survival needs. It

should also be a *vocation*, or an activity which produces a sense
of self-fulfilment, self-worth or contribution to society. While it
need not occupy all of our talent, time and energy, a career
should be conducive to our personal, professional, and spiritual
well-being. It should provide pleasure, challenge, and opportunities for personal growth.

In the chapters which follow, we will explore the many issues
involved with our career or life path, and through a deep
understanding of the messages found in the human hand, we
will be able to direct ourselves in an area or areas that will help
bring about personal integration and help us achieve our
highest potential.

Chapter 2

YOUR CAREER AT YOUR FINGERTIPS

Of all the aspects of the hand, the shape, size, fingerprint patterns and relative position of the fingers on the hand offer a wealth of information about our individual personalities and possible career directions. In fact, many hand analysts believe that the fingers alone can tell us more about the person and their lifestyle than any other aspect of the hand.

Each finger has a specific meaning in palmistry, and reflects the type of energy that is channelled through it. With the exception of the thumb, the fingers are named after celestial bodies, which are in turn named after Greek or Roman gods. They represent aspects of our character that are symbolized by these mythological beings.

Before we proceed to more detailed information, the essential meanings of the fingers are as follows:

The Thumb: The thumb relates to our ego strength, willpower, and our level of energy. Because it permits us to accomplish a wide variety of tasks in daily life, the thumb also symbolizes our ability to express this energy to the world.

Jupiter: The Jupiter or index finger shows our degree of self-confidence. From a study of its size and shape, we can evaluate the potential for leadership ability, ambition and the desire to succeed in life.

Saturn: The Saturn or middle finger reveals the serious side of our psychological nature, and is the finger of propriety, responsibility and introspection. Depending on how it is developed, this finger will reveal business acumen, reliability and steadiness, or if undeveloped, a careless or frivolous nature.

Apollo: The Apollo or ring finger is the symbol of our creative and artistic qualities. The development of this finger is associated with a talent in the field of the graphic arts (including drawing, design and architecture), the fine arts, and acting. Some palmists believe that Apollo is also related to successful careers in public speaking, advertising and public relations.

Mercury: The Mercury or little finger reveals our ability to communicate. Our capacity to express ourselves through writing, acting and speaking can be reflected in this finger, as well as our talent for business, sales, commerce, languages and broadcasting.

When studying the various fingers, it is important to consider each finger both by itself and also as an integral part of the hand. In addition, we must also understand the relationship of each finger to others. We can determine the finger's relative strength by opening the palm completely with the fingers held together. If the fingers tend to lean towards one in particular, that finger is the dominant finger of the hand and provides us with the keynote of the individual's character. The hand in Figure 2.1, for example, reveals a strong Saturn influence.

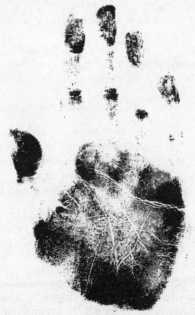

Figure 2.1: Hand revealing dominant Saturn influence.

Before we discuss the characteristics of each finger, it is important to become familiar with the appearance of the fingers in general.

Flexibility: The degree of flexibility of the fingers provides important clues to the person's character and its ability to adapt. Ideally, the fingers on the hand should arch gently backward under pressure, revealing a capacity to adapt to new ideas and situations.

Length and Width: The length of the fingers must be judged in relation to the length of the palm. A balance would exist when the fingers are in proportion to the length of the palm itself.

Generally speaking, people with *short fingers* (Figure 2.2) are quick thinkers. They tend to be impulsive and instinctual, and are able to grasp quickly the essential points of an issue. They also view things on a large scale, be they philosophical concepts, sales strategies, or specific tasks to accomplish. Unless their fingers are knotted, they tend to overlook details and can be less than thorough in completing assigned tasks.

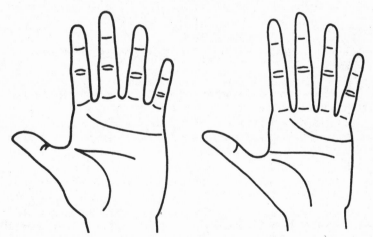

Figure 2.2: Hand with short fingers.

Figure 2.3: Hand with long fingers.

Long fingers (Figure 2.3) indicate opposite qualities. Owners of long fingers tend to fuss over small details and like to focus on the minutiae of daily life. Long fingers often promote an introspective nature, and suggest analysis, patience and thoroughness.

People with *thick, fleshy fingers* have a basically sensate nature. They enjoy luxury, good food and sensate pleasures, and are sometimes drawn to careers like cooking and catering.

Thin fingers tend to reveal a more intellectual person, who is often removed from the trials and tribulations of the three-dimensional world. Careers in research, library science, writing and computer analysis would be favoured by people with thin fingers, especially if they are long.

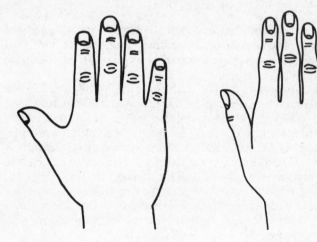

Figure 2.4: Hand with smooth fingers.

Figure 2.5: Knotty fingers.

Knuckles: The shape of the fingers has nothing to do with overall intelligence, but has much to reveal about the type of thinking a person may do. *Smooth fingers* (Figure 2.4) have an absence of developed joints, and belong to people who use intuition rather than pure reason when making decisions. Artists, poets, actors, public relations people and individuals involved with sales are the sort of people who would normally have smooth fingers. Owners of smooth fingers often have difficulty breaking down a problem into its component parts, and their decisions are based primarily on hunches rather than on careful analysis. If the fingers are smooth and short, impulsiveness, impatience and aversion to detail will be accentuated, while long fingers will tend to promote intellectual and analytical tendencies.

Fingers with joints or 'knotty fingers' that are not caused by arthritis (Figure 2.5) show a person with a strong analytical mind. Their owners often gravitate towards careers in science, engineering, and systems analysis, although this analytical component is often brought into use in a wide variety of professions. They are rarely seduced by appearances, and tend to penetrate deeply into an issue using logic and careful attention to details.

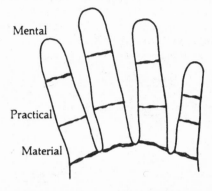

Figure 2.6: The three phalanges of the fingers. Mental, Practical, Material.

The Phalanges: The index, middle, ring and little fingers of the hand are divided into three parts or *phalanges* (as seen in Figure 2.6). The top phalange is that of mental order, the middle phalange is that of practical order, while the bottom phalange is called the phalange of material order.

Long top joints on all fingers show a thoughtful person, and indicate that mental activities absorb most of the person's attention. A long middle phalange on all fingers shows skill in business and other practical types of work. A long and thick phalange of material order reflects a person who is very grounded in the material or instinctual side of life. If other confirming signs are present on the hand, a thick phalange of material order can indicate greed or self-indulgence. Pinched in, thin bottom phalanges are an indication of fussiness. Remember that the comparative length of the phalanges may vary from finger to finger, and would influence the significance of each individual finger.

Fingertips: The tips of the fingers come in four basic shapes, and each shape denotes a special 'key quality' of the personality. Since most hands have a combination of these types, we need to take into account the qualities governing each individual finger as well as the finger's basic form.

Square fingertips (Figure 2.7) show a lover of careful, neat work. People with square fingertips respect order and regulations, and like to follow a set method in the tasks they perform.

They are practical, rational and realistic in their approach to life.

Spatulate fingertips (Figure 2.8) tend to splay outwards in the form of a spatula. They reveal a person who is energetic, down to earth, and who loves physical activity and the outdoors. Spatulate fingers also reveal intuitiveness and an entrepreneurial nature, and unless modified by other aspects in the hand, the ability to take risks.

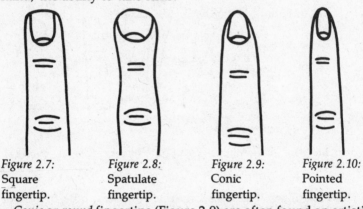

Figure 2.7:
Square
fingertip.

Figure 2.8:
Spatulate
fingertip.

Figure 2.9:
Conic
fingertip.

Figure 2.10:
Pointed
fingertip.

Conic or *round* fingertips (Figure 2.9) are often found on artistic people and others who respond easily to outside stimuli. The person is active yet receptive, mental yet emotional. Owners of these fingertips have an easy-going way of doing things.

Pointed or 'psychic' fingertips (Figure 2.10) are somewhat rare. They reveal strong tendencies of being affected by the outer environment, and show a dreamy, intuitive or inspirational type of mind. People with pointed fingertips tend not to be very practical, and tend to experience difficulty living in the everyday world.

Finger Spacing: When the fingers are held closely together on an open hand, the person has a tendency to be introverted and fearful, often lacking independence and self-confidence. He or she would tend to conform to the rules and not wish to 'rock the boat', both in the workplace and in their personal affairs. The wider the spacing between the fingers, the greater the openness, daring and self-confidence. Very extroverted people – including small children – will put their hands on the table with all of their fingers splayed outwards.

When there is a gap between the Jupiter and Saturn fingers, there is an ability to make decisions for yourself and those around you. This feature can often be seen on the hands of managers and other decision makers, rather than those in executive positions who are not actually making the day-to-day decisions. Strictly speaking, this is not a sign of leadership, but rather one of *initiative:* the ability to decide what to do, when and how to do it.

A gap between the Saturn and Apollo fingers usually occurs only when the fingers are widely spaced. It shows independent thinking about the basic issues of life. The degree of space between the Mercury and Apollo fingers indicates that the person will be an independent (and often unconventional) thinker.

Fingerprints: Your fingerprints are important because they represent the most basic and unchangeable elements of your personality. Although you can learn to modify the traits they represent, you can never completely be rid of them. Doctors have named the study of these fine ridges in the skin *dermatoglyphics,* and there are several medical books which discuss their significance. Ridge lines in the skin run all over the palm of the hand, as well as the soles of the feet. In later chapters we will be dealing with some of these patterns as they relate to careers, but in this chapter we will concentrate only on those found on the fingertips.

Essentially, there are three basic types of fingerprints: the whorl, the arch and the loop. They account for approximately eighty per cent of all fingerprint patterns.

Figure 2.11: The whorl.   *Figure 2.12:* The arch.

The *whorl* (Figure 2.11) is the sign of the individualist and the thinker. A person whose fingerprints are mainly of the whorl type would tend to be his or her own person, rather than one of the crowd. He or she would tend to have clearly formed opinions, and would have the ability to keep secrets. Very often a predominance of whorls can indicate a special talent or ability that will distinguish the individual from others. Positive qualities of the whorl include those of intensity and all-round ability. Negative qualities include the tendency towards isolation and becoming too wrapped up in one's personal dramas.

The *arch* fingerprint pattern (Fig 2.12) is the sign of a practical nature. A person whose fingerprints are primarily of the arch pattern tends to be reliable, hard-working and efficient. He or she would tend to be skilled with the hands, and have the ability to make, mend or repair things. Positive aspects of the arch include consistency, realism and usefulness, while the negative aspects can include reluctance to accept change and difficulty in responding to new ideas and unexpected situations.

Figure 2.13: The loop.   *Figure 2.14:* Composite pattern.

The *loop* (Figure 2.13) is the sign of the balanced 'middle of the road' person who fits in well with others. Those with a predominance of loops on their fingertips tend to be easy-going, are good at dealing with people, and make the most of any situation. Positive qualities of the loop pattern include flexibility and all-round capability. The main negative aspect can be a lack of individualism and the tendency to conform.

While the whorl, arch and loop account for the vast majority of fingerprints, there are several less common patterns which are worth mentioning. One of these is known as the *composite* print (as seen in Figure 2.14). It is related to the whorl and is composed of two loops curling around each other. In addition to reflecting the ordinary whorl characteristics, the owners of composite prints tend to see two sides to each and every issue and often experience difficulty making up their minds.

A *tented arch* (Figure 2.15) so-called from the little vertical line in the middle which looks like a tent-pole is a sign of enthusiasm, although it still reflects the qualities of the ordinary arch. A tented arch is not just an arch with high curving ridges: it must have the little 'tent-pole' in the centre to be genuine!

Figure 2.15: Tented arch.

When studying the fingertips, remember that strong, clear fingerprint patterns intensify the meaning of each type and bring out their more positive qualities. Although not essential to our discussion here, we may come across rare cases of eccentric or strangely-formed prints which invariably accompany strange and unusual personalities. Consult Andrew Fitzherbert's *Hand Psychology* (see Bibliography) for further discussion.

Now let us consider each finger individually.

THE THUMB

Of all the digits of the hand, the thumb is by far the most important. Its size, shape, strength, expressiveness and position or setting on the hand itself reveal a tremendous amount of information about the overall strength of the personality. In Hindu palmistry, there is a complete system of analysis based solely on the study of the thumb.

The thumb is the symbol of our ego strength as well as our level of energy, drive and forcefulness. Because in reality the thumb enables us to perform a wide variety of physical tasks in daily life, the thumb symbolizes our ability to function in the world.

The size of the thumb is an indicator of our basic energy level. Normally, the tip of the thumb reaches the lower phalange of the index, or Jupiter finger. A long thumb which is fairly thick and broad (Figure 2.16) indicates an abundance of energy as well as a forceful personality. Long, strong thumbs are found on

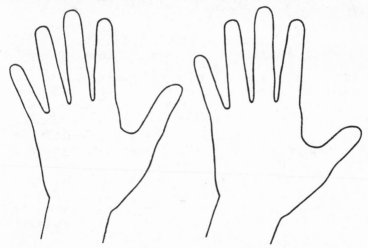

Figure 2.16: Long thumb.   *Figure 2.17:* Short thumb.

people who usually have their own way in any situation.

Individuals with short thumbs (Figure 2.17) tend to be weak-willed and are often dominated by their long-thumbed counterparts. They may also lack self-confidence, forcefulness, and the ability to follow a project or other endeavour through.

However, before we proclaim a thumb to be long or short, we need to take into account how it is positioned on the hand. A low-set thumb (Figure 2.18) can be positioned at a ninety-degree angle to the index finger. It reveals a person who is adaptable, independent, and who is inclined to take risks both personally and professionally. A thumb held closely to the rest of the hand (Figure 2.19) is an indication of a careful and generally conservative person.

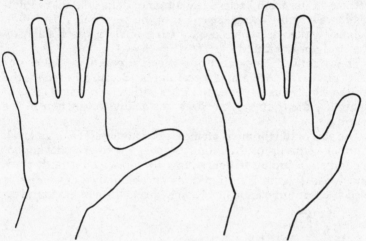

Figure 2.18: Low-set thumb.   *Figure 2.19:* Thumb set high.

A thumb that is both long and broad would be found on an individual who will try hard to achieve his personal and professional goals, and who has both the energy and force to do so. A long but fairly narrow thumb reveals the desire to achieve success, but a lack of driving force. This sort of thumb is often found on intellectuals and others who tend to work quietly and persistently in their chosen profession.

A small, broad thumb reveals a lack of 'staying power' but an abundance of energy and drive. A small, narrow thumb reveals an altogether weak personality who has difficulty achieving success. Nevertheless, it is possible that this weakness can be compensated for by a special talent or other ability.

Like the other fingers, the thumb is divided into three basic parts, as seen in Fig 2.20. The nail phalange is connected to will-

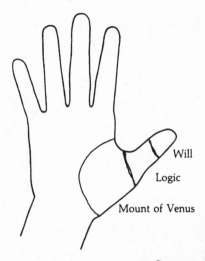

Figure 2.20: The three phalanges of the thumb.

power, while the second is known as the phalange of logic and reason. The lower part is called the mount of Venus in palmistry, and will be discussed in Chapter 4.

A strong phalange of will – one that is well-rounded, long and wide – indicates decisiveness, staying power and the ability to transform thoughts into deeds. Square-tipped thumbs reveal organizing ability and are said to indicate a sense of justice and fairness when it comes to making decisions concerning others. A spatulate phalange is a sign of physical dynamism, aggression and a fighting spirit. Conversely, if the top phalange is narrow or pointed, will-power will often be lacking and the person's energy may tend to scatter when confronted with a major project or a situation that requires long-term attention.

If the phalange of will is thin or flat (when viewed from the side) the person tends to be nervous and highly-strung. Generally speaking, thick top joints show a blunt, no-nonsense way of doing things, while a tapered tip is an indicator of a more subtle personality. A thick-thumbed person who wants to sack you from your job will tell you so immediately in no uncertain terms, while a boss with a thin thumb tip would flatter you and invite you to lunch, yet would make certain that your notification of dismissal would be waiting on your desk when you returned.

If the bottom section of the thumb is broad (it sometimes can appear to be somewhat swollen in appearance) the person will be blunt and straightforward when dealing with others. When

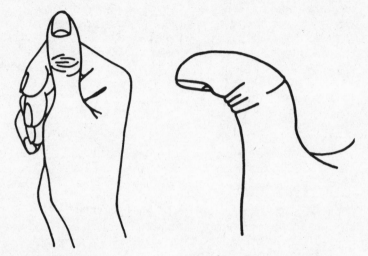

Figure 2.21: Waisted thumb.   *Figure 2.22:* Supple thumb.

the phalange of logic is 'waisted' (Figure 2.21), the individual tends to be tactful, persuasive and clever.

Ideally, both the top and middle phalanges should be the same length, indicating a balance between will and reason. A long top joint and short middle joint reveal a tendency to act without much reflection, while a long middle joint and short top joint tend to favour more thinking, more talking, and less action.

Determining the *flexibility* of the thumb is also important. A supple thumb (Figure 2.22) bends back at the joint, and indicates emotional versatility. People with flexible thumbs are changeable, adaptable and generous. On the negative side, they can be unreliable and tend to take on too many responsibilities at once. If the thumb bends back to an angle of ninety degrees or more, the tendency to be unreliable is strengthened (unless modified by other aspects of the hand) and the person can be extravagant and generous to an extreme.

The less flexible the thumb, the greater the reliability and persistence. However, if the thumb is stiff and will not bend back at all under pressure, its owner will be stubborn and have difficulty adapting to new ideas and unforeseen situations. Yet the qualities of a stiff thumb can be modified by a flexible hand.

The fingerprint on the thumb reveals how the person sets about doing things in life. A *whorl* shows an individualistic way of getting things done which may go against common or accepted practice. An *arch* indicates a sense of practicality and a directness when undertaking a project or other endeavour. A *composite* pattern betrays a habit of indecisiveness in approaching and executing projects, which could mean that they could take forever to complete. A *tented arch* combines practicality with enthusiasm, while a *loop* reveals average middle-of-the-road qualities. It is by far the most common pattern to be found on the thumb.

JUPITER

As mentioned earlier, the Jupiter or index finger is the symbol of self. It represents leadership, ambition, and the drive to succeed in life. Ideally, this finger should be the same length as the ring or Apollo finger, and should reach slightly higher than half-way up the top joint of the Saturn, or middle finger.

A long Jupiter finger reaches more than two-thirds of the way up the top phalange of the Saturn finger, and is often longer than the finger of Apollo. When this occurs, the ego is strong, with plenty of self-confidence on a deep level. The owner is sure of his or her abilities, likes to take charge, and is very concerned with self-development and personal advancement. People with long Jupiter fingers are natural leaders, and are often involved in running a business or in any job which requires administrative or executive ability.

To the degree that this finger is short – i.e. shorter than Apollo – there is a corresponding lack of self-esteem and self-confidence. There may also be a tendency to be doubtful of one's abilities and to be afraid of failure. While a short index finger may be ideal for a person who works for others, stressful work, pressure from one's boss or co-workers, and the fear of failure may indicate that self-employment (or employment in a low-pressure environment) may be a wise career direction.

Very often a shy, insecure person with a short index finger attempts to overcome their problems by becoming overly aggressive and independent. In these cases, the finger tends to jut outwards. People with this feature tend to break away from the influence of employers and co-workers and prefer to be self-employed. A hand which reveals some manual skill and a short 'independent' index finger probably belongs to a self-employed tradesperson, such as a carpenter, plumber or electrician. Salespeople often have this configuration as well. Although they may work for someone else, sales work is essentially a form of self-employment with the salesperson being his or her own boss.

To the degree that the Jupiter finger bends towards Saturn, the person tends to be insecure. This is often manifested in their lives by jealousy, possessiveness and acquisitiveness. People with bent index fingers can often be found browsing through antique shops and flea markets looking for something to add to their particular collection.

A squarish tip on the Jupiter finger betrays strong organizational and executive skills, and is often found on the hands of administrators and planners. A spatulate first finger would add a streak of dynamism to the personality, and would increase the tendency to want to take risks. A pointed Jupiter finger is a sign of inspiration. It is found on people who are attracted to mysticism, but also gives the individual an ability to inspire others and help them overcome their problems.

Fingerprint patterns will also provide important data on the qualities of the Jupiter finger, and relate primarily to one's personal interests and goals. A whorl betrays individuality, and the ability to form one's own ideas despite pressure from others. An arch pattern reveals practical ability when dealing with both personal hobbies and work. The presence of a tented arch increases one's innate enthusiasm when dealing both with personal goals and inner beliefs, while a composite print indicates indecisiveness regarding one's beliefs and goals in life. Because both sides of an issue are understood clearly, there is often difficulty in making a choice or choosing a clear path of action.

SATURN

The Saturn or middle finger denotes seriousness, and is the finger of propriety, responsibility and introspection. It serves as the link or 'balance finger' between the subconscious aspects of the personality represented by the fingers of Apollo and Mercury and the outgoing, conscious qualities of the thumb and Jupiter finger.

A long Saturn finger reaches high above the fingers on either side. It reveals a person who treats life with the utmost seriousness, and who is strongly interested in personal success. People involved in areas of scientific research, as well as businesspeople who deal extensively with money, stocks and property often have long middle fingers. When this finger is short, its owner tends to be careless and does not like to take on heavy responsibilities. For the vast majority of individuals, however, the Saturn finger is neither very short nor very long.

When the middle finger is straight, there is generally a balance between liking to work with people and preferring to be alone. When the finger curves towards Jupiter, the individual likes to be in the company of others most of the time, while a slight curve towards Apollo indicates a need to work alone more often than not.

A whorl on Saturn shows a current of individuality in one's

working life. This often leads the person to select an unusual career or an unconventional line of work. An arch reveals the ability to introduce a practical approach to one's job. A tented arch increases enthusiasm, and can enable one to complete difficult projects with increased drive and optimism. A composite fingerprint pattern tends to reveal a sense of ambivalence towards one's chosen career, and often is found on people who are endlessly searching for 'the right job'.

APOLLO

The Apollo or ring finger is the symbol of creativity on the hand. People with long and strong ring fingers are largely attracted to careers involving design, art and music. They are often found in the entertainment industry. When the finger features a spatulate tip, the ability to work with the public is enhanced, and it is often found on public speakers, actors, dancers and singers. A pointed tip indicates one's artistic sense and reveals a well-developed sense of style.

On some hands, the Saturn and Apollo fingers tend to bend towards each other. When this occurs, there is a tendency to sacrifice pleasure for duty. The person may have stifled his or her innate creativity in order to achieve financial success or to otherwise fulfil their responsibilities to others.

A whorl fingertip pattern on this finger is a sign of strong artistic skills, and is often found on painters, graphic artists and designers. An arch on the Apollo finger suggests an ability to work at a more 'sensate' form of artistic endeavour, such as sculpture, woodcarving, metalwork or ceramics. A tented arch – while rare – reveals a special enthusiasm for a particular form of art, while a composite pattern indicates a variable taste in art, which may involve constant changes in clothing styles or home decor.

MERCURY

The Mercury or little finger rules communication. Ideally, this finger should reach the top phalange of Apollo. In some cases, the little finger is set low on the palm, which may make it appear shorter than it really is. If this is the case, place the Mercury finger of one hand over the Apollo finger of the other to determine its proper length. The longer the Mercury finger, the greater the ability to communicate with others. A high proportion of successful writers, entertainers, lawyers, business people, teachers and politicians possess a long and well-developed Mercury finger. It is also found on people with above average intelligence.

A short little finger can be an indicator of difficulty in relating to other people. Those who have it are often inclined towards emotional immaturity and have trouble relating to co-workers as other adults. While in some cases this quality may have its advantages (people with childlike qualities are often very appealing to others) owners of short Mercury fingers often have difficulty in their intimate relationships.

For the most part, a little finger which is carried sticking outward from the hand indicates emotional or sexual problems. When held very close to the rest of the hand, it is a sign of a conformist in both a social and sexual context.

Most people have all finger joints on Mercury of equal length. A very small minority possess two joints instead of three, which indicates a trend towards highly unconventional or even deviant behaviour. The presence of four phalanges (also quite rare) has the same meaning as a long Mercury finger. In the normal three-sectioned finger, a short and often narrow second phalange is commonly the sign of poor organizing skills.

To the degree that the Mercury finger is straight, the greater the honesty, frankness and trustworthiness. A slight curving towards Apollo reveals a degree of shrewdness, and is often found on successful businesspeople and political figures. Mariano Ospina Perez, President of Colombia (1946–50) managed to lead his highly vulnerable government through one of its most turbulent and chaotic periods in history. The owner of a very strong thumb and a long and slightly curved Mercury finger, his diplomacy and sagacity earned him the nickname of 'The Silver-haired Fox'. When this finger bends sharply towards Apollo (naturally and not as the result of arthritis or an accident) there is a tendency to manipulate others and to be dishonest in order to achieve one's goals.

The Mercury finger nearly always bears a loop fingertip pattern, unless all the other fingerprints on the hand are of another type. It is rare to find an isolated print on this finger, so no certain interpretations can be laid down. However, when the Apollo and Mercury fingers are marked with whorls – and if the fingerprints on the other fingers are another type – the person's subconscious mind is unusually active. This can lead to precognitive dreaming, as well as hunches and mental impressions of all kinds.

A NOTE ABOUT NAILS

Although the fingernails are primarily of value in medical diagnosis, they can also help evaluate character when it comes to choosing a career path or direction. Ideally, the nails should

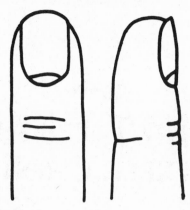

Figure 2.23: Normal nail.

be slightly curved as opposed to flat, as seen in Figure 2.23. People with long nails are often drawn to artistic pursuits, and they like to think and analyse. Narrow nails reveal a narrow, dogmatic outlook on life which allows little room for innovation or the acceptance of new ideas. Broad nails reveal broad-mindedness. Short nails (when not the result of nail-biting) indicate an impatient and often critical personality. Although not the easiest people to work with, owners of short nails make excellent quality control inspectors and can be relied upon to locate the weak points of any idea, product or corporate strategy.

Chapter 3

HAND TYPES AND CAREER CHOICE

As the shape and overall appearance of the hand is a primary indicator of our overall personality, a careful and thorough understanding of the various hand types is essential for an accurate vocational hand analysis. The easiest way to determine the hand's basic shape is to trace an outline of the hand onto a piece of paper using a ball-point pen or sharp pencil. Very often the shape of the hand will relate to the types of lines and type of fingerprint patterns the hand carries. It can also reveal important information regarding the kind of work you (or the person whose hands you are analysing) may be best suited for.

Over the years, many hand readers have sought to classify the hands into distinct categories. While no single system is perfect, classifying the hands provides a basic framework around which we can build a thorough vocational hand analysis.

The system of hand shapes we will be using in this book was introduced by Fred Gettings in his classic work *The Book of the Hand*. It is favoured by many palmists due to its reliability and ease of practical application. The Gettings system is based upon the fact that the palm can be long and narrow (i.e., rectangular in shape) or short and wide, which gives the hand a squarish appearance. Because the fingers of the hands can either be long or short, four basic hand types are produced.

The names of the four types are taken from ancient alchemical writings, and correspond to the four elements: Earth, Water, Fire and Air. Like the traditional names for the fingers and mounts of the hand such as Jupiter, Saturn and Mercury, these four names are both useful and easy to remember. Some hand analysts have tended to move away from these names in order to appear more modern, while others have invented new names of their own. We prefer to use the time-honoured names for the mounts and fingers. For the four hand types, we believe that it is best to use the standard names which Gettings determined.

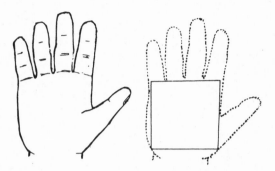

Figure 3.1: Earth hand.

THE EARTH HAND

The earth hand (Figure 3.1) reveals a basically square palm with short fingers. Earth hands usually contain very few lines, and it is common to find arches or low loops on fingertips.

People with earth hands are often very grounded in three-dimensional reality, and work well in the material world. They tend to be slow, careful and practical, and prefer to see things in a simple, uncomplicated way. For the most part, the owner of the earth hand dislikes change, and prefers a stable and predic-table job with few, if any, surprises. People with earth hands often like to concentrate on one major activity throughout their working lives. Careers in agriculture (such as farming), mining, working with heavy machinery, and similar work involving strong physical labour are popular. Because they tend to be more attuned to nature, earth-handed people prefer to live and work in the country rather than in cities or towns.

Occasionally, an earth hand will contain one or two strange markings in the skin ridges or the lines. Gettings called these 'evolved earth hands'. This can indicate that besides the essential 'earth' qualities, other modifying factors exist, such as a special talent or better-than-average intelligence.

Most earth hands appear to have a long little finger. However, since the fingers on most earth hands tend to be short and stub-by, the Mercury finger only *appears* to be long in comparison to the rest. For that reason, the little finger should not be inter-preted as it would on a more 'average' hand.

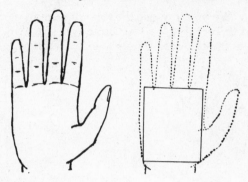

Figure 3.2: Water hand.

THE WATER HAND

The palm of the water hand (Figure 3.2) is rectangular, and the fingers tend to be long. In addition to the four major lines on the hand, there are usually a great number of fine lines, including lots of vertical lines. This type of hand is especially common among women.

Because people with water hands tend to be quiet and not very aggressive, they tend to gravitate towards professions which enable them to express their innate sensitivity, refinement and good taste. They are often influenced by other people and outer circumstances.

Women with water hands are often attracted to the classic 'feminine' occupations like modelling, retailing (especially in areas of fashion and interior design) and office work. The female water hand is also found on many beauticians and make-up artists, especially when they work for others. Low-pressure jobs involving books (such as certain types of library work and retail sales in smaller bookshops) may also be indicated.

The water hand reveals a thoughtful or intellectual person. Men with water hands tend to be thoughtful and studious, and like women, gravitate towards jobs in retail sales, modelling, office work (such as working as a clerk or word-processor operator) and library research. Because water-handed people often lack aggression, they are usually promoted on their own merits rather than on the ability to take advantage of whatever situations come their way.

Extremely feminine women, particularly fashion models and some actresses, often have exaggerated forms of the water hand. Like the hand of Faith Brown, the noted British impressionist (Figure 3.3), such hands are very long and thin, and give the impression of being both delicate and sensitive.

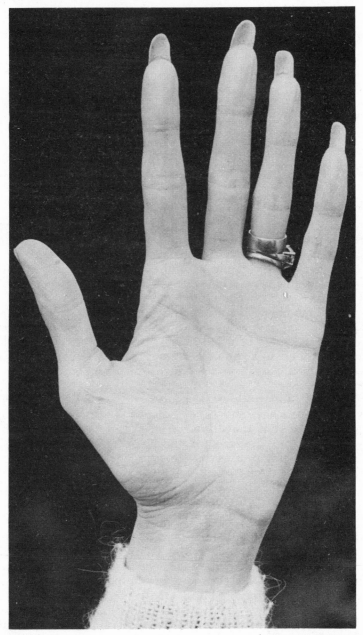

Figure 3.3: The hand of Faith Brown. (photo: John Shelton courtesy of *The Sunday Mirror*.)

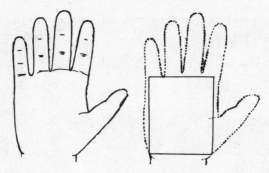

Figure 3.4: Fire hand.

THE FIRE HAND

When we look at the fire hand (Figure 3.4) we can see that the palm is rectangular and the fingers are short compared to the size of the palm itself. There are always a large number of strong, clear lines engraved onto the palm, revealing both energy and intensity. Whorl fingerprints are the most commonly found among owners of fire hands.

Unless modifying factors are present in the hand, people with fire hands are nearly always extroverts and are exciting to be with. They tend to be active, always on the go, and find it difficult to adhere to a particular routine. They are emotional and excitable, and like to exert an influence on other people and control situations.

Owners of fire hands are best suited for careers which involve adventure, change, and positive assertion. Unless modifying factors are present, they thrive on stress and have the ability to get things done. Craftspeople, businesspeople, entrepreneurs, people in helping professions (i.e., massage therapists, nurses, physicians and other healers), police officers, firemen, dancers, designers and skilled manual workers often possess fire hands.

THE AIR HAND

The palm of the air hand (Figure 3.5) is square, and the fingers are long – at least as long as the palm itself. The fingerprints often feature loops (usually high loops) and the lines on the palm are usually long, clear and well-formed. However, these long lines are often quite thin.

People with classic air hands are mentally alert, curious, and like to learn. They tend to be attracted to learning how ideas and things fit together. They like to see connections between ideas and events.

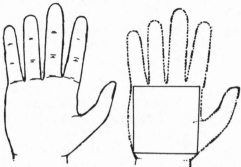

Figure 3.5: Air hand.

Three features stand out about air-handed people:

1. They are insatiably curious.
2. They love to express their ideas and opinions.
3. They look for connections between things, and want to know how isolated facts fit together into the whole picture.

Owners of air hands often enter professions which involve communication. Writers, public relations people, broadcasters, artists, dancers and teachers tend to have hands that are of the air type. Because air-handed people tend to be emotionally stable, they can often be relied upon.

For a beginner to palmistry, the air hand is often the most difficult to recognize, and amateur palmists often misidentify it. If you seem to be having problems making a classification, look for the high loops on the fingerprints and the long, thin lines on the palm of the hand.

Approximately three-quarters of the hands you will read will definitely fit into one of the four hand types described in this chapter. This will leave a small number which are more difficult to classify. Sometimes the shape of the hand may be of one type, but the lines or fingerprints belong more to another. Such a hand belongs to a person with a more complex or mixed personality, and should be analysed accordingly.

A very small minority of hands simply cannot be classified at all. Perhaps the fingers are neither long nor short, or the palm itself may be indeterminate in shape. If this is truly the case, one must assess each separate feature of the hand as it is, without attempting to classify the hand into one of Gettings' four types. Such hands definitely test one's skill as a hand reader! However, for the great majority of hands, the Gettings system is a very useful tool for career guidance and character analysis.

CONSISTENCY

The consistency of the hands is determined by measuring their hardness or softness under pressure. Understanding the basic consistency of the hand helps us determine the level of energy the person has, and how it can be expressed in the workplace. By taking your friend's hands in yours and gently squeezing them, you can gain an accurate idea about their consistency.

The flesh of a *flabby* hand easily crushes when you squeeze gently. People with thin, flabby hands have low physical energy and are not very inclined to work unless they are strongly encouraged to do so. When they interact with others in the workplace, they often have difficulty expressing their feelings and can give the impression of being emotionally 'flat'. In general, flabby hands are an indication of the idle, sensitive dreamer who dislikes both physical and psychological exertion. Unless modifying aspects are present in the hand, or unless owners of thin, flabby hands make a sustained effort to overcome lethargy and lack of motivation, prospects for a successful career are rather slim.

When the hands are flabby and thick, the person will be more sensual and can tend towards laziness. If the thumb is small, or if it bends back easily, will-power is often lacking, and it can be difficult to carry out assigned tasks.

Soft hands show a lack of bony feeling under pressure. While soft hands can also reveal a low energy level, they offer more potential than a flabby hand does.

Elastic hands cannot be easily crushed by your grasp and tend to spring back under pressure. They reveal a person who is adaptable, and has the ability to respond easily to new ideas, unforeseen situations, and a variety of challenges at work.

Firm hands are slightly elastic and yield to moderate pressure. People with firm hands like to be active at work, tend to be emotionally stable, and can be relied upon to fulfil their responsibilities. However, they may also have difficulty adapting to new ideas and unexpected situations, and may tend to want outer events (as well as co-workers) to adapt to their particular vision of things. However, with time, they can change their point of view.

Hard hands do not yield under pressure, and are often coarse in texture with no elasticity. People with hard hands have an abundance of physical energy and are perfectly suited to work involving physical exertion, such as farming, mining, lumbering, factory work and building construction. They are tough, single-minded people who have a tendency to be set in their ways. In addition, they are often prone to 'hold in' their energy, which could result in sudden outbursts of temper.

FLEXIBILITY

Hand flexibility can be determined by the ease with which it bends backwards under pressure, and reveals both our ability to adapt to unexpected situations and to be open to new people or ideas.

A *very flexible hand* can bend back to nearly a ninety-degree angle with a minimum of pressure. It reveals a person who is impressionable, easily ordered around by others, and who may have difficulty sticking with one activity at a time. Unless the modifying influence of a rigid thumb is present, owners of very flexible hands can be unreliable and are prone to be unpredictable in their thoughts, feelings and actions.

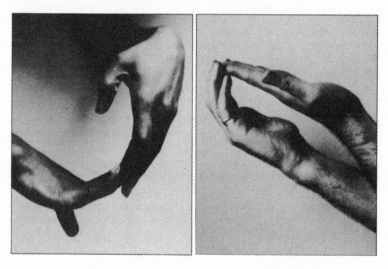

Figure 3.6: Moderately flexible hand.   *Figure 3.7*: Stiff hand.

A *moderately flexible hand* bends back in a graceful arc, as seen in Figure 3.6. The owner of this type of hand has the ability to adapt fairly easily to new ideas and unforeseen situations. While it may be easy for such a person to feel, think and act, there could be the danger of taking on too many responsibilities without being able to successfully carry them out.

A *firm hand* hardly bends back at all under pressure. Owners of this type of hand tend to be stable and focused in the workplace, and can be relied upon to get things done. Although people with firm hands are open to new ideas, they are rarely

impulsive and often have difficulty adapting to new circumstances and unfamiliar surroundings.

A *stiff hand* (Figure 3.7) is extremely rigid, and may actually
turn inwards in its normal state. Although this hand reveals a
person who is extremely cautious, highly responsible and
dedicated to hard work, people with stiff hands are often stubborn, set in their ways, and find it extremely difficult to respond
to new ideas and unexpected situations. Because owners of stiff
hands tend to be secretive, they may have difficulty sharing
their feelings and problems with others. However, if a particular
task at work involves a degree of confidentiality, people with
stiff hands can be relied upon to keep quiet.

HAND SIZE

The relative size of a person's hand is another indication of
character. It can be determined in the context of the person's
overall size, including height, weight, and bone structure.
Generally speaking, *small hands* reveal an individual who views
life on a grand scale. People with small hands tend to perceive
the totality of what interests them, rather than its component
parts. Unless modified by other factors (such as knotted fingers)
there can be an aversion to detail and the need to learn how to
patiently proceed step-by-step towards accomplishing one's
goals.

People with *large hands* appear to gravitate more towards small
things. They tend to be more mental than instinctual, and can be
very thorough in their approach when dealing with
philosophical or technical concepts and challenges found in the
workplace in general. Large hands are often found on watch-
makers, mathematicians, surgeons, engineers and others who
are drawn to detailed work.

Unlike the apparently contradictory aspects of large and small
hands, narrow and broad hands reveal corresponding aspects of
the personality. *Narrow hands* reveal a narrow, restricted way of
looking at life, which is accentuated if the hands are inflexible
and hard. People with narrow hands would be drawn to careers
which are eminently respectable, and which do not require innovative thinking or unconventional approaches when dealing
with problems or other issues. Conversely, *broad hands* reflect a
person who is open-minded, tolerant, and interested in new
concepts and trends. People with broad hands and wide spaces
between the fingers are drawn to work involving innovation,
creative thinking, and an unconventional approach when dealing with new products, challenges and situations at work.

SKIN TEXTURE

The texture of the skin also corresponds to one's emotional nature. The softer and finer the skin, the greater the degree of physical and emotional sensitivity. Coarse skin texture reveals a more 'rough and tumble' individual who is not strongly influenced by his or her surroundings. We are often asked whether the work that one performs determines skin texture. Although certain physical labour can produce callouses and may tend to coarsen an otherwise fine textured hand, we have found people with coarse textured hands whose most strenuous task was punching a computer keyboard, while we have seen owners of fine textured hands operating heavy road-building equipment.

WHICH HAND IS WHICH?

When we analyse a person's hands, we need to discover which of the two is the dominant hand. The non-dominant or *passive hand* reflects our past and our innate potential, while the dominant or *active* hand reveals what we are doing with our lives at the moment. To use the analogy of banking, our passive hand would be compared to our stocks, bonds, securities and other non-liquid holdings, while our active hand would represent our short-term savings and current accounts. Both can change over time, but like savings and current accounts, the active hand appears to reflect changes in our lives more rapidly than the passive hand. Very often, the hands reveal marked differences between our innate potential and the degree to which this potential is being fulfilled.

Generally speaking, the dominant hand is the hand we write with. In the rare instances when a person is ambidextrous and writes with both hands, we should ask questions as we proceed with the reading in order to determine which of the two hands is the more dominant one.

Chapter 4

HAND TOPOGRAPHY: THE MOUNTS

The palm of the hand is not quite flat. There are numerous pads of muscle and flesh on the hand which give the palm an irregular appearance that is unique to every individual. The topography of the hand can be likened to that of the countryside. The various pads can be likened to hills and valleys, while the lines of the hand can be compared to rivers flowing between them.

Figure 4.1: The apex of the mount.

Traditional palmistry has called these pads *mounts*. A great deal of information was written about them in times past, but unfortunately much of this information is either inaccurate or incorrect. There is some controversy, for example, about the number of mounts on the hands. Traditional Western palmists have taught that there are four mounts under the four fingers. At the centre of each mount is a convergence of skin ridges known as the 'apex' (Figure 4.1). These mounts were given the astrological names of Jupiter, Saturn, Apollo and Mercury.

However when we count the mounts according to actual pads

of flesh, we can find only three. Hold your palm out at eye level. Look along the palm from wrist to finger as if you were sighting along a barrel of a gun. You will easily see three pads in between the four fingers, making three mounts rather than four.

Ancient Chinese palmistry also counted three mounts under the fingers, and called them 'palaces'. The Palace of Wind (the self) is located between the index and middle fingers, the Palace of Separation (employment and authority) is located between the index and ring fingers, while the Palace of Earth (beauty) can be found between the ring and little fingers.

In this chapter we will continue to use the four traditional names. Just remember that although there are four areas called 'mounts', they do not correspond to the actual pads in a living hand. A diagram of the hand which includes the four traditional mounts can be seen in Figure 4.2. Don't be concerned if you do not have a mount in each of these places. Some hands hardly have any mounts at all, while others have only one or two that are really prominent.

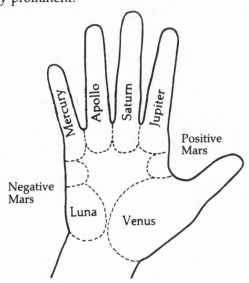

Figure 4.2: The mounts of the hand.

When doing a careful hand analysis, we need to consider whether the subject's palm has strong mounts or not. The presence of many prominent mounts is a sure sign of enthusiasm, while a very flat hand reveals a lack of vitality. This comparison will highlight the differences between a person who lives life to the full, and the individual who never gets very excited or involved in anything and whose life is generally boring and bland, with very little passion or excitement of any kind. As you will discover by observing many hands, most have a mount pattern that lies somewhere in between these extremes. Nevertheless, if you find a person with prominent mounts – or someone with no strong mounts at all – the interpretation mentioned here is very reliable.

Flat-mounted people are suited to quiet, unadventurous jobs. Their most favoured occupations would include clerical work, office work, and any jobs which provide a basic, reliable routine involving little emotional or physical exertion. People with flat mounts seldom possess much physical stamina, and have little or no desire for an exciting and stressful work environment.

By contrast, the woman or man with full mounts is often unsuited to quiet work. Travel appeals. People coming and going are a source of interest and pleasure. Constant, varied activity and a sense that things 'need to be done' are also common among people with prominent mounts. These people work best when given a variety of tasks and plenty of work to do.

The three pads between the fingers tend to develop equally, so if one is prominent, the others will probably be also. For this reason, it is perhaps more useful to study the strength of each finger itself rather than the prominence of the mounts that lie between them.

Nevertheless, we do need to look for certain marks and signs on the mounts which provide valuable information about character and possible career directions. These signs are of two types: *markings in the skin* and *patterns of lines,* such as crosses, squares and stars.

The skin markings are called *dermatoglyphics.* They are the tiny ridges which form the skin itself. The entire palm is covered with patterns of these tiny corrugations which are unique for every individual. These skin ridges extend upwards to the tips of the fingers, where they form fingerprints. They cease at the wrist where the ridged skin of the palm gives way to the ordinary skin of the arm.

The best way to see them is to study the palm under strong light. Bright sunlight is the best of all, although a good lamp will do. You may also wish to use a magnifying glass. Another good way to study dermatoglyphics is to take prints of your hands as described in Chapter 15, so that you can study them at your leisure.

One of these skin patterns is of special interest to us in our study of mounts. As mentioned earlier, the convergence of skin ridges under each finger creates what palmists have called an apex, and its location provides important information about career and self-fulfilment.

Figure 4.3: The apex of Jupiter.

THE MOUNT OF JUPITER

The most interesting of these apexes is the one found under the Jupiter finger. Ideally, it should be positioned exactly under the middle of that digit (Figure 4.3). In some hands it is slightly displaced towards the thumb, while in others it tends to veer closer to the middle, or Saturn finger.

When the apex is displaced towards the thumb, it is said to be located on the *radial side.* Although rare, it reflects daring, independence, and a dislike for convention and authority. It is found on people whose actions tend to be unpredictable and unexpected.

There are few 'standard' jobs for such people. All too often they wind up in unconventional professions which can sometimes border on illegality. Figure 4.4 shows the hand of a young prostitute, who took up her profession after finding it impossible to hold down a conventional job. The apex on the radial side has also been found on drug smugglers. It is not a mark of criminality *per se,* but is a sign that its owner is definitely unsuited for stable and regular occupations. These men and women need freedom, adventure, and genuine challenge in their working lives. Possible jobs for these people would include those of stunt person, explorer or expedition leader, mercenary, professional wrestler or boxer, or even work in criminal investigation, espionage, or military intelligence.

Beryl Hutchinson, the respected English palmist and author of *Your Life in Your Hands,* found this mark among members of the families who had pioneered farming in Australia, New Zealand and Africa. Many present-day descendants of these pioneers have inherited this mark. Ms. Hutchinson herself had it, as her

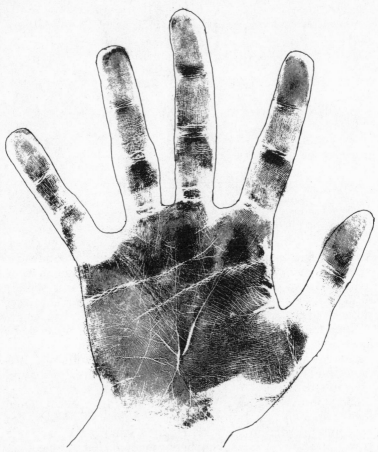

Figure 4.4: Misplaced apex.

love of adventure would indicate. She was awarded the MBE (Member of the Order of the British Empire) for her work in Kenya during the dangerous Mau Mau uprising in the 1950s.

An apex on the radial side of Jupiter can occasionally be found on the hands of people in fairly ordinary jobs. Invariably, such people still display a strong independent streak both at home and at work. The occasional business executive and entrepreneur may have this mark, and lawyers have been known to have it as well, particularly those who specialize in defending major criminal cases. Individuals who engage in almost any kind of pioneering activity, including innovative people working in the fields of advertising, design and film-making, may well have this marking in their hands.

A more common variation is for the apex of this mount to appear on the other side (the ulnar side) bringing it closer to the mount of Saturn. It is a sign of caution. The owner of this mark dislikes taking risks. He or she is generally cautious, restrained, and likes to play it safe. There are no specific jobs that are related to this pattern. However, those who have it tend to stick to their jobs. They often spend many years in the same line of work and are reluctant to change either their occupation or employer.

This pattern often accompanies a curving index finger, which we described in Chapter 2. It is also commonly found with tied head and life lines and tied life and fate lines, which we will discuss in Chapter 5. All of these signs reflect a cautious and restrained personality.

What if the apex of this mount is located directly under the Jupiter finger? When this occurs, a sense of balance exists between the extremes described above, and the person is able to integrate a sense of adventure and unconventionality with responsibility in his or her working life.

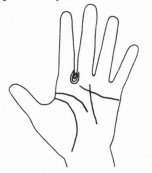   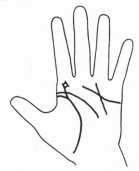

Figure 4.5: Raja loop.   *Figure 4.6:* Teacher's square.

One hand in twenty shows a loop pattern between the Jupiter and Saturn fingers, as seen in Figure 4.5. This is known as the *Raja loop* or *loop of charisma*. A fine marking to have, it goes with the ability to take the lead, to rise to the top, or to earn respect and admiration from others. Leaders in many fields, including politicians, radio and television personalities, and successful entertainers, often feature a raja loop in their hands.

Raja loops are also found among gurus and other spiritual and religious leaders. People who set out to gather disciples while teaching their brand of spiritual truth often have the loop of charisma. There are cases of people of low morality and little spiritual ability who have successfully played 'guru' for years on the strength of the charisma loop in their hands.

Anyone with a raja loop can succeed at anything requiring public success or winning votes. The only time it can be a disadvantage is when the individual wants to remain unknown or inconspicuous. A bank robber with a charisma loop would probably have a very short career. An individual working for an agency like the CIA or KGB might find it a disadvantage as well.

The mount of Jupiter sometimes bears two small patterns which are none the less very important. The first is known as the *teacher's square*. It consists of a distinct square attached to a line which rises vertically from the life line (Figure 4.6). This mark is related to a strong capacity to teach. It is very common among gifted teachers, as well as those who worked as teachers before moving on to other careers. Anyone who has this small marking can excel in giving lectures, running classes and presenting workshops. In some cases, it goes with the ability to write textbooks and training manuals. The teacher's square often accompanies other marks that are connected to healing and counselling. They will be discussed in detail later on in this book.

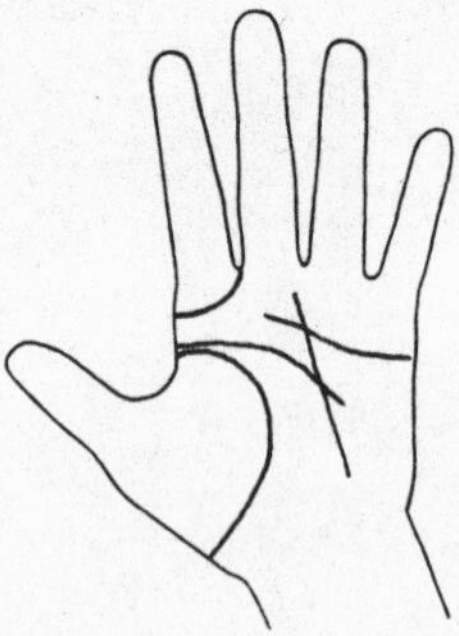

Figure 4.7: Ring of Solomon.

Another interesting marking on the Jupiter mount is the *ring of Solomon* (Figure 4.7). A clear and well-formed ring of Solomon is often considered to be a sign of mystical inclination. It is often found on clairvoyants, seers and mystics. In fact, it indicates psychological insight, and is a sign of ability in the fields of counselling and therapy. For this reason, it can sometimes be found in the hands of psychotherapists, career and marriage counsellors, and many types of healers, especially those involved in alternative or unorthodox therapies.

MOUNTS OF SATURN AND APOLLO

The mounts of Saturn and Apollo are of relatively little importance in our discussion on palmistry, career and self-fulfilment.

There are traditions in palmistry which maintain that the Saturn mount is connected to such occupations as mining and farming, and professions associated with death, such as those of under-taker and public executioner. The Apollo mount has long been associated with the arts, including painting, music and poetry.

Early palmistry books placed a good deal of importance on the height of these mounts and their 'inclination' towards each other. However, because the muscular pads do not lie under these mounts but between the fingers, these rules are open to question. Perhaps an occasional specialist may have a cross or star on one of these traditional mounts to reveal his or her pro-fession. It is possible that the public executioner really did have

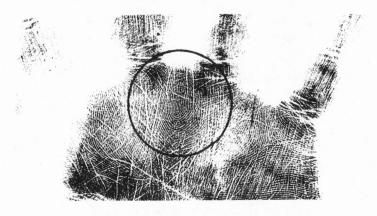

Figure 4.8: Loop of Seriousness.

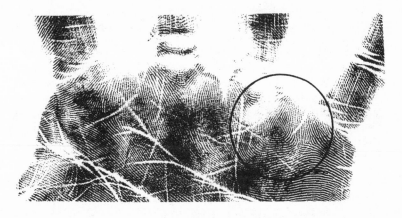

Figure 4.9: Loop of Humour.

a cross on the pad under the Saturn finger. Somewhere in the archives of palmistry there may be an opera singer with a star on the pad under the Apollo finger. However, such markings are extremely rare and are often grounded in little more than superstition. They should not be taken seriously.

However, the skin ridge patterns *between* the mounts of Saturn and Apollo are very important indeed. Many people have a distinct loop between the middle and ring fingers (Figure 4.8) while others have a similar loop between the ring and little fingers (Figure 4.9). The former is known as the *loop of seriousness*, while the latter is called the *loop of humour*. These loops can vary in their size and clarity. Occasionally you will find a very large, clear specimen, while at other times you will have to look very closely (often with a magnifying glass) in order to find any loop at all. Both loops are linked very strongly to one's aptitude for work in general.

The loop of seriousness is found on a person who has a responsible and serious attitude towards life and work. The loop is very common among businesspeople, as well as others who are involved in areas of research, teaching, banking and healing. Students with this loop study hard. Businesspeople with this loop make money. Writers with a loop of seriousness finish their manuscripts on time. The presence of a clear and well-defined loop is a reliable indicator of material success.

The loop of humour has an opposite meaning. People with this loop often value comfort and enjoyment above proficiency and financial reward. They tend to be light-hearted, like to work at their own pace, and be in an environment that suits them. A very high proportion of part-time workers and self-employed people have the loop of humour in their hands. Interesting jobs that do not necessarily pay well are often favoured by those with this loop, as are jobs in which the rules are not too strict or well-defined. There is nothing inherently lazy about people with a loop of humour, although they do not have the hard, 'driving' quality that is generally associated with the loop of seriousness.

The loops of seriousness and humour reveal our basic attitude towards life, and affect everything we do. Employment is just one of these areas, so it shouldn't be considered as something apart from the rest of one's basic attitudes towards life. There are times when we may read the hands of a person with a loop of seriousness who is chronically unemployed, or an individual with a loop of humour who has earned lots of money. However for the most part, a well-defined loop of seriousness is a reliable indicator of a steady job with good prospects of material success.

When both loops are developed in the same hand, we have a

person who has both a serious approach to life and an ability to be relaxed and enjoy himself at the same time. Such people can take on almost any kind of job and make a success of it. The presence of both loops is a very favourable pattern!

THE MOUNT OF MERCURY

The mount of Mercury lies directly under the little or Mercury finger. The most interesting marking on this mount that relates to career is known as the *medical stigmata* (Figure 4.10). It is composed of a group of small vertical lines (also known as 'samaritan lines') isolated from any other small lines which may be scattered about under the finger. The medical stigmata received its name through being found in the hands of some medical doctors. It is also found among nurses, therapists, chiropractors and others who are involved with healing and counselling. It shows not only an interest in helping and caring for others, but often genuine healing ability. While it is certainly possible to succeed in a healing profession without this mark, there is no doubt that those who have it can excel at medicine and health-related fields.

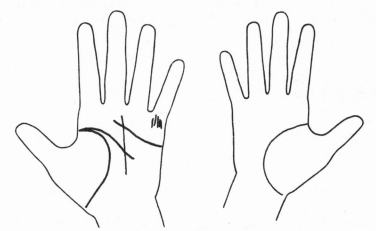

Figure 4.10: Medical stigmata.

Figure 4.11: Life line forming broad arc around Venus mount.

THE MOUNT OF VENUS

Ideally, the mount of Venus comprises the ball of the thumb and is outlined by a widely sweeping life line. The normal mount should take up approximately one-third of the palmar surface, and should neither be too hard nor too soft.

Although few specific career choices can be based on this

mount alone, it is a prime indicator of our basic level of vitality. A weak and flabby mount reveals a low level of energy, while a firm, high mount of Venus reflects plenty of energy and drive. People with a weak mount of Venus are often unsuited for strenuous physical work, while those with a strong mount tend to be more outgoing, exciting, and enjoy physical and emotional challenge in their job.

Sometimes the Venus mount appears to be very large because the life line, which marks the boundary of the mount, swings out into the palm in a wide curve (Figure 4.11). This pattern is a sign of an abundance of physical strength, and is often found on the hands of professional wrestlers, weight-lifters, dancers and others with good physical skill.

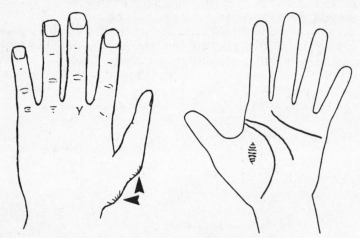

Figure 4.12: The angles.   *Figure 4.13:* The bee.

Strictly speaking, the mount of Venus is actually the third joint of the thumb, fused into the palm. People with a strong musical talent invariably have strongly marked lower joints in this part of the palm (Figure 4.12). These joints are known as *the angles*, and are found on almost all professional musicians. Although there are other indicators on the hand which reflect musical ability, the angles are by far the most important.

Skin ridge patterns on this mount can also reflect a musical person. In particular, a pattern known as *the bee* (Figure 4.13) is sometimes found on people with a special ability to play string-ed instruments. Many professional guitarists and violinists have this sign, as do others who have never learned to play, but none the less feel a special attraction to music played on stringed instruments.

THE MOUNTS OF MARS

Just above the mount of Venus where the web of the thumb appears, is the location of the mount of Mars. In the average hand, this area appears to simply be part of the mount of Venus. In a few hands, a distinct and separate pad of flesh can be found here which often appears like a callous.

Most traditional palmists believe that every hand has a mount of Mars. Because this mount often appears weak or flat, perhaps it would be more accurate to say that only a few hands actually possess it.

When present, this mount reveals a courageous and fighting spirit. Those who have it are willing to fight for what they believe in. As can be expected, the mount of Mars is often present on hands of those who make their careers in the military. Firemen and police officers often have a well-developed mount as well. A well-developed mount of Mars has been found on a surprising number of social workers and on people who run homes and shelters for the sick and the homeless. Katherine St. Hill, who was President of the London Cheirological Society in the 1890s, noted that nuns who provided social services in the city's most poor and dangerous neighbourhoods often possessed a strong mount of Mars.

Traditional maps of the hand show two mounts of Mars. The mount described above is called *Mars Positive*, while the other, which lies directly opposite on the outer edge of the hand, is called *Mars Negative*. This mount has often been linked to the ability to resist aggression, and its presence is said to be a sign of staying power and resistance. Because there is no separate pad of flesh to outline this particular mount, some palmists feel that there is little evidence to support its meaning. However, a number of palmists who study past and future events from the lines of the palm believe that legal conflicts and military adventures can be marked on this mount.

THE MOUNT OF LUNA

The lower edge of the palm which lies opposite Venus is the mount of Luna. As the seat of the subconscious, it is the realm of dreams, fantasy, imagination, and extra-sensory perception. A well-padded mount of Luna often reveals a strong imagination, and is found on many writers, inventors and artists.

However, more important than the padding are the marks and other signs found on this mount. If the head line runs down onto this mount, the mind will be preoccupied with imaginative matters, as shown in Figure 4.14. This is by far the most telling

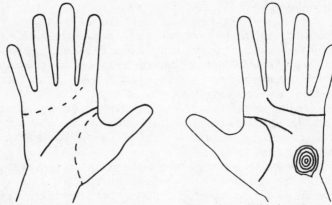

Figure 4.14: Head line dropping strongly towards Luna.

Figure 4.15: Whorl on Luna.

sign of creative imagination. Designers, script-writers, copy-writers and others whose work involves strong imaginative talent all tend to have this line/mount configuration.

A whorl pattern on the mount of Luna (Figure 4.15) reflects a strong ability to visualize. Although rare, it can be observed from time to time in the hands of artists. It would be a useful marking for an architect, playwright, or any person whose work demands the ability to communicate visions and impressions to others.

A loop coming from the outer edge of the hand onto the mount (Figure 4.16) indicates a strong affinity with nature. It is especially common among people involved in agriculture, including farmers, beekeepers, environmentalists and water diviners. Although this loop is not strongly linked to any kind of

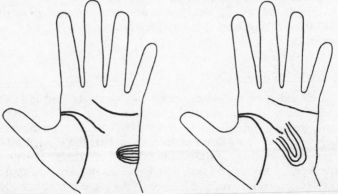

Figure 4.16: Loop from other edge of hand.

Figure 4.17: Loop from inside of Luna towards edge of hand.

particular employment, those who have it always have a 'feel' for the natural environment and are often drawn to careers or hobbies that are related to nature.

A loop on Luna running the opposite way (i.e., from the centre of the palm onto the mount as seen in Figure 4.17) is an indicator of psychic awareness and telepathic ability. It is extremely common among clairvoyants and other psychic people of all types, including card-readers, mediums and psychometrists. Astrologers and palm-readers are prone to having this loop as well, including those who swear that their work is entirely scientific and has nothing whatever to do with ESP. Small lines that run diagonally up this mount from the wrist area have also been linked to intuition and psychic ability.

Sometimes the mount of Luna swells outwards so that the lower corner of the palm bulges into a prominent curve. This is known as the *sailor's pattern*. Nearly everyone who possesses it in their hands will have a strong attraction to the sea. The majority of sailors and those who choose a naval career will have this formation. The telepathic loop described above is often found on a mount of this type as well.

There is also a rare *S-bend pattern* (known also as a composite print) that can occur on the mount of Luna. Males who have this marking are inclined to be gentle and sensitive. They virtually never choose jobs that involve strenuous physical labour, aggressive sales, or any work that demands aggressive behaviour. Women with this pattern tend to show the reverse characteristics, and often become tough business negotiators and decisive executives and leaders. The lone woman on the board of directors of an engineering firm, for example, may well have this pattern in her hands.

Chapter 5

HAND TOPOGRAPHY: THE LINES

The lines of the hand indicate the major talents and energies we have at our disposal, our capacity to manifest these talents in our life, and the possible directions in which these talents and energies will lead us. In essence, the lines of the hand form a natural map of the course of our life, and have much to reveal about career path and self-fulfilment.

It is important to remember that the lines of the hand can change over time, and are affected by both attitude modification and changes in behaviour. The most noticeable changes often occur in the hands of people who lead eventful, interesting lives, as well as in those whose minds are more open to the world around them. Although we have seen major lines change in as little as four weeks, the most marked changes in the lines take place over a period of a year or more. For those who are interested in achieving their full potential, the objective knowledge offered by the lines of the hand can be highly valuable as well as exciting. The lines reveal that we are indeed the 'master of our fate' and can assume personal responsibility for our lives and career direction.

As seen in Figure 5.1, there are four major lines in the hand as well as approximately a dozen minor lines and markings. Because we will be mainly concerned only with those lines which have a bearing on career and self-fulfilment, we will not be discussing the meaning of all the lines here. For those who want to deepen their knowledge of the lines in the hand and their meaning, a more detailed examination is included in *Hand Psychology* and *The Palmistry Workbook* as well as in other books we have listed in the Bibliography.

Basically speaking, the *life line* reveals our level of physical

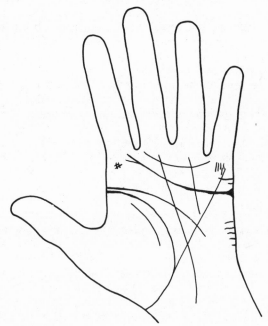

Figure 5.1: Major lines of the hand.

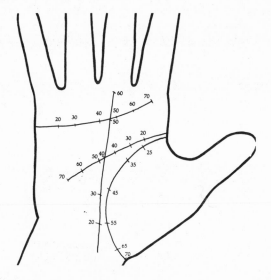

Figure 5.2: Gauging time on the major lines of the hand.

strength, stamina and energy. Because we can also estimate time on the hand (Figure 5.2), this line can also record periods of disease, accidents and other events which touch our life.

The upper transverse line or *heart line* reveals our emotional and sexual nature. It reveals the quality of our feelings, and our capacity for love and affection.

The lower transverse line or *head line* reflects mental abilities. It can also indicate our way of looking at the world and can point out periods of emotional difficulty and any accidents or injuries which may affect the head.

The *fate line* or 'line of destiny' reveals primarily our psychological attitude towards our work or life path. It indicates our level of personal success as we see it, as well as recording the obstacles, changes and other influences which challenge us during life.

The major lines in the hand should be clear and well-defined, and have a colour which complements the skin. The width and depth of the lines should be equal. When a line is particularly strong and deep, excessive energy is often present, while a broad, weak and shallow line indicates a lack of focus and strength. A hand with deep, strong lines (especially when the fingers are splayed out) often reveals a high achiever. An abundance of lines in the hands (in addition to the major lines) indicates hypersensitivity and nervousness, while only a few lines are an indication of little sensitivity and few basic channels for life expression.

Before we examine the major lines involving career and life direction, there are several important line formations we need to

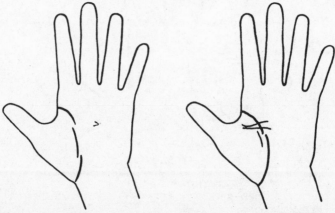

Figure 5.3: Splintering or splitting of a line.   *Figure 5.4:* Lines of influence.

keep in mind. When a line *splinters* or *splits* (Figure 5.3), the line's strength and focus are dissipated. In some cases (especially on the fate line) a split can indicate a change in career or a new phase in life, so it should not be read as negative.

Lines of influence (Figure 5.4) are tiny lines which can either cross or run parallel to the major lines. Generally speaking, when they cross a line they indicate traumas, obstacles or dramatic influences or events in the person's life. When they run parallel to a line (particularly when it is broken) they tend to strengthen the defective line that is islanded, broken or chained.

Islands (Figure 5.5) occur when there is a splitting from a line which joins the line later on. For the most part, islands impair the strength of a line and indicate a lack of focus (especially

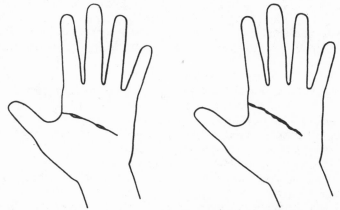

Figure 5.5: Islands.   *Figure 5.6:* A chained line.

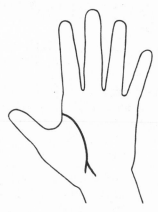

Figure 5.7: A forked line.

when found on the lines of head or fate) and dissipation of energy. A *chain* (Figure 5.6) is composed of many islands tied together, and can indicate a tendency for long periods of scattered or unfocused energy.

A *fork* (Figure 5.7) appears at the end of a line when the line splits. Depending on where it appears, a fork can indicate a division of one's energy or focus, or can be a sign of balance and adaptability, especially if it occurs on the heart or head lines.

THE LIFE LINE

The life line is the principal line of the hand, and is our primary indicator of the strength of our physical constitution and basic level of vital force. It begins at the edge of the palm between the thumb and index finger and sweeps downwards towards the wrist around the ball of the thumb. Because it relates primarily to health and not to career, it will not be dealt with in any great detail here.

However, the deeper and clearer the line, the stronger the physical constitution and greater the energy to devote to one's chosen profession. In contrast, islands on the life line can reveal periods of weakness or ill health, which can also have an impact on both the direction and success of one's career. In some cases, excessive stress on the job can be manifested as a period of weakness on the life line. By the same token, a serious accident or illness recorded on the life line can have a dramatic influence on one's career path.

Most of the marks found on or beside the life line relate to events which take place during one's life. A 'sister' life line running next to the life line provides it with added strength, and lends support – both physical and psychological – during periods of illness, stress or other difficulty.

When the life line forms a broad arc around the mount of Venus (Figure 5.8), the person tends to be energetic, warm and emotionally responsive. When the life line moves close to the thumb, cutting through the Venus mount (Figure 5.9), the person will tend to be rather cold and unresponsive. If the life line is weak as well, and the mount of Venus somewhat flat, the person's energy will tend to be low. This is important to understand, because so many people fail to realize that this problem may be a major cause of poor performance at work, as well as of other difficulties regarding career direction and commitment.

When the life line moves away from the ball of the thumb towards the mount of Luna (Figure 5.10), the person will have a restless disposition and may be drawn to an occupation which involves a great deal of travel.

Figure 5.8: Wide arc around Venus.

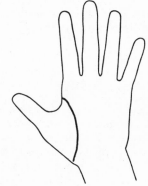

Figure 5.9: Life line cutting through Venus.

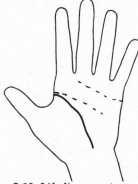

Figure 5.10: Life line moving Towards Luna.

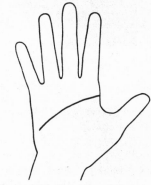

Figure 5.11: Long head line.

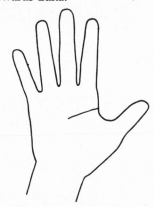

Figure 5.12: Short head line.

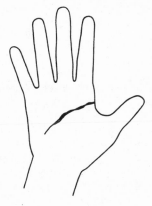

Figure 5.13: Chained head line.

Though it does not directly relate to our discussion on careers and palmistry, one final comment must be made regarding the length of the life line. A short line of life is not necessarily an indicator of an early death, nor will a strong, long life line guarantee that its owner will live to a ripe old age.

THE HEAD LINE

The lower transverse line or head line begins at the line of life and moves horizontally across the hand. While some palmists feel that the head line is an indicator of intelligence, this line primarily reveals the *way* we think. It shows both the type and class of intelligence the person has at his or her disposal.

A 'good' head line is clear, and free of islands, breaks and frets. It should slope gently downwards and end with a small fork (known as 'the writer's fork'), denoting a balance between realism and imagination. The average head line ends somewhere under the Apollo finger.

A *long* head line (Figure 5.11) indicates that one's thinking is careful, detailed and comprehensive. There is often a wide range of intellectual interests as well. A *short* head line (Figure 5.12) does not mean that the person is short on intelligence, but rather is an indicator of a person whose thinking is simple, practical and to the point. Thought processes are limited primarily to mundane affairs.

If the head line is *chained* (Figure 5.13) the person has a sensitive, highly strung personality and can be especially prone to stress. Stress can also be seen by tiny frets on the head line, or a head line with a 'woolly' appearance. When the source of stress is removed, or if the person learns how to deal with it creatively, symptoms of stress on the head line will probably disappear. Chains on the head line may also indicate a tendency to be mentally scattered and unfocused.

One or two islands on the head line (Figure 5.14) reveal that the person may crack under intense emotional pressure or severe stress. It may also be an indicator of psychological disturbance which requires professional help.

A *wavy* head line (Figure 5.15) reveals an original (and often unusual) mind which can conceive of new ideas and unconventional points of view. A *straight* head line (Figure 5.16) may either run across the hand, or can slope downwards. It indicates clear and concentrated thinking regardless of the direction in which it moves. A *curved* head line (Figure 5.17) reveals a mind which likes to experiment and play with new ideas.

When the head line moves straight across the hand, it reveals a practical, realistic and analytical mind, which always sees the

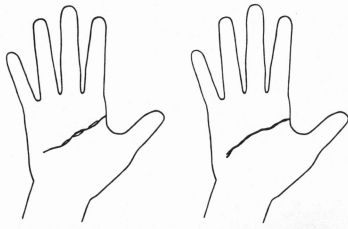

Figure 5.14: Islands on head line.   *Figure 5.15:* Wavy head line.

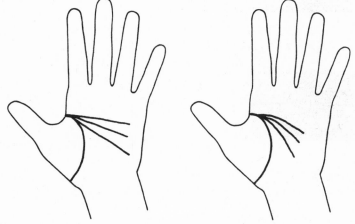

Figure 5.16: Straight head lines.   *Figure 5.17:* Curved head lines.

practical side of a problem or situation. Conversely, a head line which slopes downwards betrays a good imagination and a creative intellect. The more profound the slope, the greater the imagination. We have often seen short, sloping head lines on the hands of engineers and others who deal with mechanical and practical matters. They view things in a more concrete way, despite their creative turn of mind.

A *fork* at the end of the head line shows the capacity to see more than one point of view. Because many writers have been found to have this formation, it has become known as the 'writer's fork'.

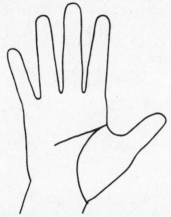

Figure 5.18: Life line connected to head line.

Figure 5.19: Life line separated from head line.

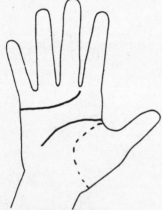

Figure 5.20: Wide space between head and heart lines.

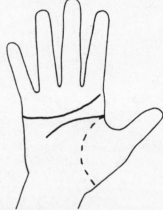

Figure 5.21: Narrow space between head and heart lines.

When the head line is joined with the life line at its commencement (Figure 5.18) there is a tendency to be cautious and careful, and the individual will tend to be hesitant to take risks. The more strongly tied these lines, the greater the caution and the reluctance to act independently. In general, the point at which these lines separate indicates the age of psychological independence from parental influence, whether real or imagined.

Widely separated lines (Figure 5.19) belong to impatient, impulsive people who tend to make their minds up quickly. They are often extroverts who are accustomed to taking risks. Separated life and head lines are often found on those who learned to think for themselves at an early age.

When there is a wide space between the lines of head and heart (Figure 5.20), there is a broadminded, unconventional and more 'open' type of personality. When the space between these lines is narrow (Figure 5.21), the person tends to be narrowminded, repressed and secretive, especially if the life and head lines are strongly joined.

THE HEART LINE

The upper transverse line or heart line is the emotional barometer of our lives. Moving from below the Mercury or little finger across the palm, it reveals the quality of our emotions, our degree of sensitivity, and our capacity for love and affection.

Generally speaking, people with long heart lines which end at least under the Jupiter finger tend to be ruled more by their emotions than intellect. If the heart line is straight and long, it is the sign of the humanitarian (especially if the line is chained, revealing strong sensitivity). A short heart line ending under Saturn would reveal an individual who is run more by the head than the heart. A straight heart line (Figure 5.22) runs horizontally below the fingers. It betrays a more 'mental' type of lover. Such a person can be cool and thoughtful in matters of love, and can be prone to repressing what are often intense feelings.

A curved heart line (Figure 5.23) is found on a 'physical' type of person, who is more active than receptive, and more physical in expressing feelings than people with mental heart lines. While the heart line will reveal itself primarily in relationships, it may also be applicable to career decisions.

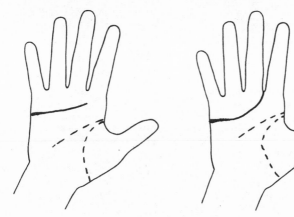

Figure 5.22: 'Mental' heart line.   *Figure 5.23:* 'Physical' heart line.

A person with a long, chained, 'mental' heart line would probably not be fit for jobs involving high levels of stress, cut-throat decisions, and a work atmosphere which demands insensitivity and hard-heartedness. For example, a property-developer with such a heart line would probably find it very difficult to evict a group of elderly tenants in order to build a new high rise block of flats, unless he or she was certain that they would have alternative housing. A property-developer with a short and more insensitive heart line would tend to be far more concerned with profit margins than with the welfare of others. For this reason, long, straight and sensitive heart lines are especially common among therapists, healers, counsellors, social workers and others who are interested in helping others.

However, since the hand reveals primarily the underlying aspects of the personality, no hard and fast judgements should be made. There may well be people with short heart lines who are indeed very caring, while owners of long and chained heart lines have been known to be both cruel and aloof. They often repress their feelings of compassion in order not to appear vulnerable and 'soft-hearted' to others.

THE SIMIAN LINE

The so-called simian line exists when both the heart and head lines join together as one. It appears as a straight line across the hand (Figure 5.24). As the simian line tends to intensify both the mind and the emotions, any kind of job which requires high energy – whether physical, mental or psychological – would be favoured by people with simian lines. Unless modified by other

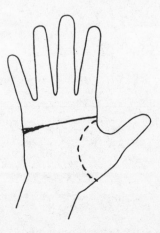

Figure 5.24: Simian line.

aspects of the hand, people with these lines have tremendous drive and tenacity, and often thrive in careers that are physically active or mentally demanding.

THE SATURN LINE

The line of Saturn (which is also known as the 'fate line' or 'line of destiny') is essential to our study of palmistry and career development. While the various mounts and fingers of the hand are important guides to career direction, the Saturn line reveals our psychological attitudes towards our work, and the type of work patterns which suit us best.

The line of Saturn normally begins at the base of the palm between the mounts of Venus and Luna, and moves upwards towards the Saturn or middle finger. It may be long, short, crooked or straight. The longer and clearer the line of Saturn, the more settled the direction of our life. Rather than a sign of outer success, the meaning of this line is more subjective. If a wealthy, outwardly successful executive is unhappy with his or her vocation, the fate line would probably be weak or fragmented. By the same token, the person who cleans the executive's office every night and is happy with his or her career, may have a long, deep and clear Saturn line.

A long, straight line of Saturn (Figure 5.25) that runs up most of the length of the palm reveals a person who is very set in his or her career direction. This is why, in the past, this line was seen as a sure sign of a successful career. However, long and clear Saturn lines can also be found on people whose careers are

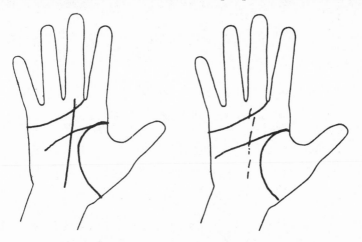

Figure 5.25: Strong Saturn line.   *Figure 5.26:* Weak Saturn line.

in a rut, and who never seem to break out into new areas of work or interest. A housewife who has spent forty years cleaning her house may have such a Saturn line, while people who are chronically unemployed and even living in the street have been found to have strong and clear fate lines as well. They are often inwardly committed to their particular life path and have little or no interest in making dramatic changes in their lives.

Because a long destiny line reflects primarily one's attitudes, it is unwise to predict with certainty that its owner will follow only one career path through life. He or she may be prone to doing so *psychologically*, but other circumstances may interfere with employment direction despite the individual's preferences.

Weak Saturn lines, such as that in Figure 5.26, belong to less settled, unstable people. There is often a struggle to fulfil one's career ambitions. Frustration and lack of focus in life are common.

When the fate line begins at the base of the hand, the owner settled into his or her life path at an early age. For example, a woman who knew what type of career she wanted as a teenager – and then became trained in that career to begin working upon leaving school – will often have such a destiny line. Conversely, Saturn lines which begin well above the wrist belong to people whose early adult years are more varied and flexible, with the tendency to be involved in a number of career directions.

Sometimes the fate line is closely tied to the life line at its commencement (Figure 5.27). This is a sign that the person experienced a restricted or dominated childhood, and was often pushed into a particular career path by parents. The influence of

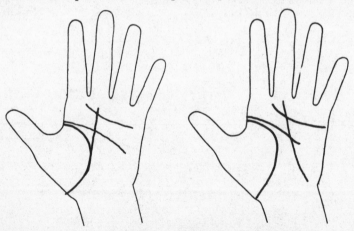

Figure 5.27: Fate line rising from life line.

Figure 5.28: Saturn line commencing in Luna.

one's parents on career direction is especially found when the fate line actually begins *inside* the life line. Fate lines that are tied to life lines are often found in the hands of people who spend their early adult years struggling to establish themselves in a career path of their own choice.

A Saturn line which commences in the mount of Luna (Figure 5.28) is often seen on people whose career involves working in the public eye. Doctors, teachers, dancers, politicians, and entertainers are especially likely to have this type of destiny line. Some palmists feel that a Saturn line emanating from Luna is an indication of a varied life path, with the potential for several different careers and frequent relocations.

A fate line which stops at the head line is often found on individuals who tend to lose their sense of direction or purpose by their late thirties or early forties (a period often referred to as 'the mid-life crisis'). They are inclined to 'drift' professionally during the latter half of their life, or will tend to experience ongoing dissatisfaction with their chosen occupation.

Most Saturn lines terminate at or near the heart line, which would indicate a traditional period of employment with subsequent retirement. However, a line which clearly runs almost to the middle finger indicates the ability to remain active into one's later years. The print shown in Figure 5.29 is that of an agronomist who joined the Peace Corps upon retirement. Until his death at the age of eighty-two, he continued to be active in theosophical studies, his masonic lodge and his church, as seen by the three small branches at the end of his fate line.

When the fate line ends deep in the mount of Jupiter, the career may involve leadership of some kind. When the line runs into the heart line in such a way as to extend the fate line to the Jupiter finger (Figure 5.30), the person can become involved in their career to the point of obsession. Though rare, this type of line can be found primarily in the hands of specialists.

Islands on the destiny line reveal a need for greater focus in both energy and ideas, while breaks on this line reflect periods of transition and possible lack of career direction.

Two or more Saturn lines (Figure 5.31) are found in the hands of those who pursue two or more careers (or one career and an important avocation) at the same time. When there is an abundance of weak parallel career lines – such as four or five – there may be a tendency to scatter one's energy in too many directions.

Sometimes you can find a broken fate line with a small parallel line next to it. The presence of this 'sister' line helps strengthen the destiny line, and tends to minimize the challenge or difficulty the broken line represents.

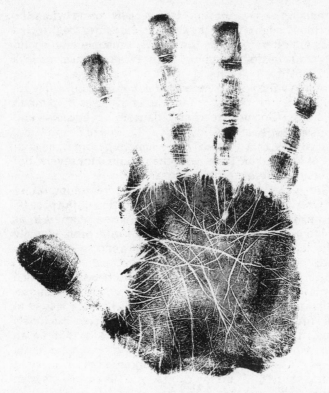

Figure 5.29.

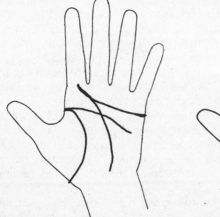

Figure 5.30: Fate line joining heart line.

Figure 5.31: Two Saturn lines.

Sometimes the Saturn line is absent altogether. When this occurs, the individual will tend to lack stability and focus in his or her career, and will be unlikely to ever settle into a set pattern in life. This commonly results in the person taking on numerous jobs for short periods of time, or jobs with frequent relocations.

In a good hand, an absent fate line can be indicative of a life involving many careers, most of which can be handled successfully. This commonly results in a life that is both adventurous and unconventional.

However, on a poor hand (i.e., a hand with poor finger, dermatoglyphic and line formations) the lack of a destiny line can almost always indicate a drifter, a drop-out, or even a criminal who has no roots and little chance of success. The degree of ability – as well as will power – revealed in the rest of the hand will help determine whether the person is an aimless vagabond or a successful entrepreneur with his or her fingers in many pies.

OTHER MARKINGS IN THE PALM

In addition to the major lines, there are a number of special markings which can offer clues to special abilities or career possibilities.

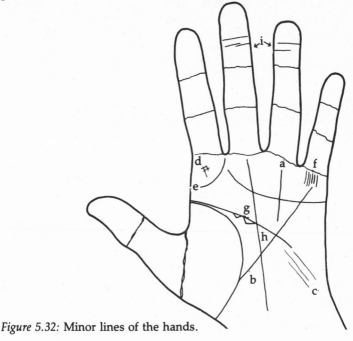

Figure 5.32: Minor lines of the hands.

THE LINE OF APOLLO

The line of Apollo is a vertical line running towards the Apollo or ring finger (Figure 5.32a). When present, it is usually short, and only rarely does it begin at the base of the hand and move up to the ring finger. While not of major significance, the presence of a clear line of Apollo has been correlated with artistic or creative ability, the capacity to make money, a flair for style, and/or the potential for fame and career satisfaction. Because such a line has been seen in the hands of many famous and wealthy people, it has been called the 'line of achievement'. However, it has also been found on people with very little fame, fortune or creative ability, although they may love music, art and other things of beauty.

THE HEALTH LINE

While of no direct impact on career, the presence of this line (Figure 5.32b) relates to our physical health and particularly that of the stomach and intestinal area. When the line is fragmented or weak, it indicates a potential for problems in this area of the body, and is found in the hands of people who are subject to ulcers, colitis, chronic constipation, parasites, and other forms of intestinal problems. Those who are involved in high-pressure jobs should be especially aware of the presence of this line in their hands, and work to minimize stress – or learn how to deal with it – as much as possible.

INTUITION LINES

Small diagonal lines which run up the mount of Luna indicate intuition or a degree of psychic ability. When the intuition line is long and continues up towards the mount of Mercury (Figure 5.32c) these abilities are accentuated. Although rare, they can occasionally be found in the hands of professional clairvoyants and very gifted psychics. Psychics often have other features, such as pointed Jupiter fingers, and the dermatoglyphic patterns on the mount of Luna we discussed in the previous chapter.

THE TEACHER'S SQUARE

A small square on the mount of Jupiter (Figure 5.32d) indicates a talent for teaching, lecturing and providing any type of instruction. While this is especially applicable to teaching on a secondary school or university level, people with this special marking often involve themselves in private tutoring, presenting workshops and seminars or offering practical instruction in subjects like swimming, yoga or crafts.

THE RING OF SOLOMON

As discussed earlier, the ring of Solomon (Figure 5.32e) consists of a diagonal line (often in the form of an arc) passing through the mount of Jupiter. Traditionally this line has been linked to a strong interest in metaphysics and proficiency in the occult sciences. However, the presence of this line primarily indicates a talent for understanding people. It reveals psychological insight into other people's lives, their hopes and their dreams. Obviously, such a line would most likely be found in the hands of good palmists, astrologers and psychic counsellors, but it can also be found in the hands of capable lawyers, psychotherapists, teachers and writers. In general, the clearer, deeper and better-formed the line, the greater and more developed the talent.

THE MEDICAL STIGMATA

The medical stigmata or 'samaritan lines' is made up of a series of tiny vertical lines which appear on the mount of Mercury, as seen in Figure 5.32f. As mentioned earlier, people with this pattern are drawn to helping others and are often attracted to the so-called 'helping professions' which involve some type of healing or counselling. In addition to medical doctors, this marking is common among nurses, massage therapists, spiritual healers, naturopaths, chiropractors and psychotherapists. It is important to remember that some medical doctors, for example, who are attracted to a career in medicine primarily to attain money or prestige, will not have the medical stigmata. It appears primarily in the hands of people who are sincerely interested in helping or assisting in the healing of others for its own sake. The hands of healers will be discussed in more detail in the following section.

When we look at the lines of the hand in relation to career direction and self-fulfilment in life, we must remember that no one is a victim of the universe and that we are each responsible for the quality of our lives; with each one of us having a specific task or tasks in life and a goal to accomplish.

Because the lines of the hand can change over time, understanding their unique message can guide us towards becoming aware of our hidden talents and aspirations, and enable us to bridge the gap between our inner desires and outer reality.

TRIANGLES

There is an additional line pattern which is somewhat difficult to describe, as it consists of strong triangular shapes anywhere on the palm. Every hand will have a few triangles somewhere, and hands with many lines may have quite a few. However, an occasional hand will reveal one or more very clearly-marked and well-formed triangles.

These triangles are seen primarily on or near the head lines of people who are technically skilled or trained (Figure 5.32g). Astrologers, tarot readers and palmists often possess the type of triangle located in the region of Figure 5.32h. Because triangles can be found very easily on the hand, it is important not to be too hasty in forming conclusions about them. However, clearly-formed triangles – especially when they stand out on the hand – are the mark of a highly-trained or skilled individual.

Another minor marking consists of lines or creases across the fingertips (Figure 5.32i). These are called *bar lines* and can come and go in the hand regularly. They are related to frustration at work, and are often found on the fingers of people who feel continually thwarted with their careers. These lines may also be accompanied by tiny frets on the head line, or a head line that takes on a 'woolly' appearance. These are all indicators of frustration and stress, and are signs that the individual should begin to deal constructively with their stressful situation rather than accept things as they are.

PART II:
FINDING YOUR SPECIFIC CAREER DIRECTION

Chapter 6

ABLE HANDS

If your palm is broad and your fingers are short, chances are that you are reading this book somewhere in the countryside. Perhaps you are sitting under a tree, or are out on the verandah of your country residence. As far back as 1843, Captain Stanislaus D'Arpentigny, the founder of modern palmistry, noticed that country people often had short, broad hands. His observations are still valid today. This type of 'able hand' reflects an individual with a strong affinity with nature, so it is not surprising that so many people who have it decide to make their home well outside the city limits.

In the 1960s, the distinguished English palmist Fred Gettings determined that the country hand usually features a squarish palm with short, stocky fingers. He named this the *Earth hand*. It is one of the four types of hand described in Chapter 3.

You may expect that such a hand would be coarse and heavy, and indeed it sometimes is. However, there are plenty of earth hands which are supple and lively, in spite of their stubby appearance. Country women often possess soft feminine hands which often conform to the 'square palm, short finger' description taught by Gettings.

The print in Figure 6.1 is a good example. To the unpractised eye, the palm may not appear to be in the form of an obvious square. However, if we measure both the length and width of the palm, we will find that they are both the same. By contrast, most palms will be longer than they are wide, producing a more rectangular pattern. In Figure 6.2, the fingers are the same length as the palm, and since the palm is short, they can be classified as short fingers.

Most people with earth hands carry their fingers quite close

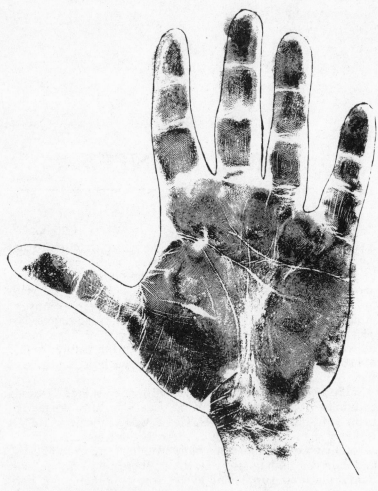

Figure 6.1: Example of an earth hand.

together. If the hand is held out, it takes an effort to spread the fingers apart. The fingers also tend to be of the same thickness from top to bottom.

Lines on the earth-type hand tend to be broader than those found on the other hand types. The main lines are often short, and there are few subsidiary (or minor) lines to be seen. The skin ridges are often strongly marked, and will stand out very clearly on an inked print. Low loop patterns are common on the fingertips, and they are often accompanied by one or more arch-ed fingerprints, revealing a very practical type of mind.

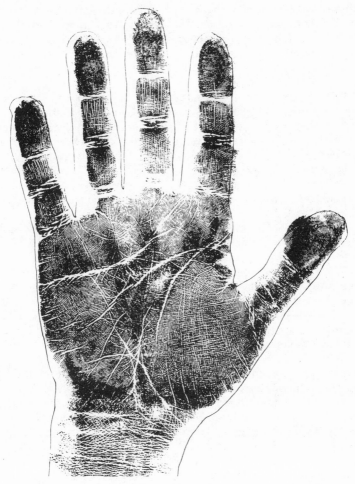

Figure 6.2: Short fingers of an earth hand.

The able or earth hand will invariably belong to a practical person, who is also the archetypical slow and steady worker. The earth-handed person does nothing in a hurry. Decisions are careful and deliberate, and opinions are formed by hours and hours of thinking things out. Actions and movements run at a similar pace. An earth-handed man doesn't bounce up from his chair and dash out of the house. He is more likely to ease himself up, say that he must be going, and then spend ten minutes getting himself ready before finally strolling out the door.

An earth-handed woman who cooks a meal will probably spend half the day getting it ready. She will then expect the entire family to sit around the table for an hour or more enjoying it. Fast foods and rushed meals are not for her. Incidentally, a very high proportion of earth-handed women (as well as many men) love to cook, and both men and women with able hands tend to enjoy large, hearty meals.

Who hasn't noticed the slow pace at which small country towns usually operate? This may be due in part to the fact that the earth-handed people who are most likely to live in or near these towns rarely can be seen hurrying down the street. Nor will you find these folk indulging in gossip and argument. They will certainly speak with you, but don't expect a rapid fire conversation. Their speech tends to be simple, direct and very much to the point, with special emphasis on the points they want to make.

Never make the mistake of assuming that people with earth hands are intellectually limited because of their quiet manner and slow pace of life. These people have the same range of intelligence as their city cousins. Some farm labourers or people working in road maintenance may have less ability than most, but the country newspaper editor, the mine supervisor or the local town council member may all have earth hands. Their minds can be as sharp as any you will find on the faculty of a major university.

Why do earth-handed people tend to congregate in country areas? It is not simply the slower, down-to-earth nature of these people which draws them to the country. There is within every earth hand person a love of the outdoors and of open spaces. The sky, the fields, the soil all exert an almost mystical pull on those with earth hands. Time and again an earth-hand person raised in the city will eventually make their way to the country. Several years back, we met a man who owned a city news agency. He sold it to purchase a similar business in a small Canadian town. Although his friends thought him crazy – his city business was very successful – they hadn't noticed his broad, short-fingered hands which drew him unerringly to his new rural home.

Earth-handed people are aware of the seasons. Like plants and animals, their lives are in tune with the natural rhythms of the year. They watch the weather. They like to be near growing things. If you know someone who is always talking about the weather, chances are that there will be strong earth qualities visible in their hands. Do you know someone who is a devoted gardener? Check out the hands. You may not find a pure earth shape, but it is probable that the lines, fingerprint patterns, or shape of the palm will reveal a strong earth element to the personality.

Two major weaknesses bedevil the earth-handed person. The first is a dislike and fear of change. The second is trouble dealing with emotional trauma. This does not necessarily mean that such people are prone to emotional difficulties. They simply have problems coping with them when they occur, especially if the hands are rigid.

Getting an earth-handed person to change can be one of the most difficult tasks you can undertake. They will stay with their farm in the face of earthquake, fire and invasion by foreign troops. They hate to move and do not like changing jobs. New technologies and new social values are greeted with deep suspicion. Although earth-handed people can accept and adapt to change, they are not happy to do so. Generally speaking, they avoid breaking off relationships, and are not inclined to develop new ones easily. For these reasons, an earth-handed person needs reassurance, support and lots of patience when major life changes need to be made.

The emotions of people with earth hands tend to develop slowly and deeply. It takes them a long time to become upset, and an equally long time for them to calm down afterwards. Emotional traumas caused by a death in the family or a marital break-up can simmer inside them for years. The earth-handed individual may remain distressed for a very long time, while others in a similar situation would have bounced back long before.

The greatest virtues of the earth hand are steadiness and hard work. A person with able hands never gives up and refuses to quit until the job is complete. You can confidently rely upon the earth-handed person to do whatever was promised. Work is taken very seriously. An individual with earth hands makes a point of doing things well, and completes each task thoroughly to the best of his or her ability. When an earth-handed person finds a suitable job, he or she will gain pleasure from doing it, and will take pride in doing it well.

Among rural workers, farmers and farm labourers form the largest groups of earth-handed people. There are no set rules about what a farmer's hand should look like other than featuring strong earth tendencies. There is no reason why a farmer should not also be a musician, a poet, or a philosopher. In these cases, the hands will vary accordingly.

The life line on earth hands may be either long or short, but it is almost certain to curve strongly out into the palm. This is a sign of strength and energy. The line is broad and deep. Although all the major lines tend to be strongly marked, the life line appears to be the strongest. The thumb is usually very rigid, as is the hand as a whole. Flexible thumbs are often found on people who have trouble sticking to things, so they would be fatal for a farmer to have.

The middle or Saturn finger is usually thick. Although its length may vary, probably every farmer has this digit strongly formed. The earlier teachings of palmistry used to associate the Saturn finger with the earth, and especially with professions like mining and farming. While the existence of a true Saturn mount is open to debate, there is evidence that a strong Saturn finger does have an association with earth-oriented activities.

The pure earth hand seldom has much of a fate line. Short, weak or featureless lines are common. They simply indicate a life that is free from much change or variety. An occasional farmer may show a long, straight destiny line running all the way up the palm. This will be more likely in the farmer who has longer hands than normal, and reveals a thoughtful nature. Very straight fate lines also indicate a stable, unchanging career. The farmer with such a destiny line is more likely to see farming as a chosen career rather than as 'something to do'.

On earth hands, fate lines which come from the outer edge of the hand are highly uncommon. It is more probable that the destiny line will be found tied to the life line at its commencement, which shows that the person is following a career that is predetermined by upbringing or by parental influence. Since many farmers come from farming families, it is not surprising that they have fate lines of this type.

A farmer who works his own farm will have signs of independence in the hand, while the labourer who works for the farmer probably will not. Independence is shown by a separation between the head and life lines at their commencement, as well as by an index finger that stands apart from the other fingers on the hand. A farmer who employs many workers may show a substantial gap between the Jupiter and Saturn fingers. Anyone who is self-employed will have at least some space between these two fingers.

We have rarely observed a farmer with a long index finger. The finger may be equal in length to Apollo, or it may be somewhat short or curved. Short index fingers indicate a degree of shyness or a sense of feeling ill at ease with others.

Farm work often thickens the skin and coarsens the fingers. This is not an inherent feature in the hand, and will start to disappear if the farmer takes a long holiday. Do not assume that a hand has to be coarse in order to take up a profession like farming. However, most people with very fine skin are not likely to take up farming in the first place, because they would probably not be drawn to strenuous physical work.

Farm labourers often have very plain hands with no special features. The typical earth shape and bare palm are all that can be expected. Very often the lines in such hands tend to be irregular, with one or two of the major lines broken into two or three pieces. There may be an odd line which appears twisted or 'strange'. Simian lines – or half-formed simian lines – are quite common. The fingerprints may contain an irregular or otherwise unusual looking pattern, or the little finger may feature very short joints or a missing joint.

There are a host of rural jobs in addition to farming which may appeal to earth-handed people. In those parts of the world where forestry is important, there is always work for skilled lumberjacks. Other possibilities include careers in conservation, road-building and maintenance, farm machinery mechanics, landscaping, and mining. Although there is no one particular feature in the hand for these types of work, signs of strength in the fingers, the thumb and mount of Venus should be expected.

Forestry workers often have longer fingers than the typical farmer. Because there is a spiritual quality to be found in most great forests, those who work there often have a touch of 'nature mysticism'. The lumberjack may cheerfully cut down a living tree, but he also has a deep reverence for nature and an appreciation of the silence in the forest. The lumberjacks we have met often have strong earthy hands that are hard, bare and contain only the major lines. However, the hand as a whole may be quite long, reflecting a thoughtful, more inwardly turned nature.

The print shown in Figure 6.3 is a good example. Although it is clearly 'earthy' in its texture and general appearance, the outline is actually that of a water hand. The palm is long, and so are the fingers. It might be called an 'earth-water' mixture, which is not a common type at all. In spite of its long shape, the hand is both broad and strong, and features a big Mercury finger typical of the earth hand. The owner of this hand is a landscape gardener. He has worked on several organic farms and is an expert on farming without the use of chemicals and artificial fertilizers.

Let us now consider the practical 'able' hands of those who find work in towns and cities. There are no general rules for such hands, but there are certainly specific features to be aware of. Arch fingerprints are found among skilled workers of all types. This does not mean that every manual worker has a full set of arch prints – just one or two arches are enough to reveal that the individual is inclined towards manual work. Although there are also excellent manual workers who do not have this

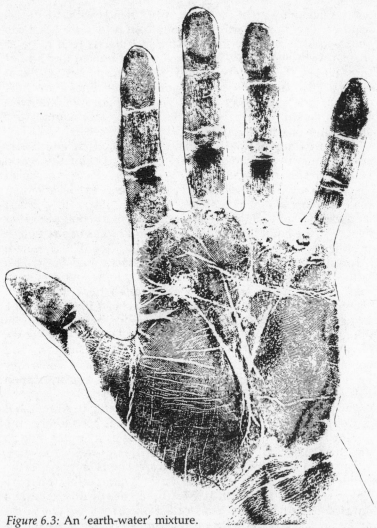

Figure 6.3: An 'earth-water' mixture.

type of print, nearly every person who has one will be bound to take up some kind of craft or handiwork as either a profession or a hobby.

If you have arches, you enjoy touching and handling things. You will also tend to have a practical mind. You also like efficiency, and you insist that machines and other objects work properly. You tend to be impatient with anything vague, useless or impractical.

If the owner of a hand with arch fingerprints is highly in-telligent, he or she will probably not choose a profession that relies totally on their manual skills. Many an intellectual with arch fingerprints may dabble in carpentry, leatherwork or book-binding as a hobby. But if the person's IQ is average or below, it will be probable that the person will choose a profession in which they work with their hands. Of course, there is nothing to stop an intellectual from pursuing a career involving manual skills, although few choose this path.

A full set of arch fingerprints can often be found on a skilled specialist. Such complete sets are rare and invariably accompany an unusual and distinctive personality. We have seen a top car-toonist with such a set, as well as a stage designer and a watch-maker. The few people who have complete sets of arches tend to be very bright and often express their manual skills through a hobby rather than a career. A full set of arches would reveal that the individual's career will undoubtedly be different, specialized, and highly demanding.

It is far more common to find a manual worker who has 'arch dominant' hands with only several arch fingerprints. The arches could be found on the thumb and the first and second fingers, with loops or whorls on the rest. In some hands, the Jupiter and Saturn fingers bear arches while the ring finger has a loop curv-ing up to look like an arch. In this case, the little or Mercury finger will invariably reveal a loop print.

A single arch print on just one of the fingers must be carefully interpreted. It will usually be on the first finger. Here, the arch qualities manifest more personally, so that the owner's hopes, goals and ideals are not necessarily work-related. The person will use his or her manual skills at home, but is unlikely to make a career of them. The psychological aspects connected with hav-ing the arch print on Jupiter will be manifested by the efficient, practical and sensible approach the person will bring to his or her job.

A single arch on the Saturn finger is frequently found on the hands of a skilled manual worker, despite the presence of an in-tellect with which the person could attain other career goals. We have seen several cases of bright women running cleaning ser-vices who could have easily taken on more mentally demanding work. Two of these women had an arch print on the Saturn finger. The other was what is called 'arch dominant', with the arch print on her index, middle and ring fingers. An individual with an arch fingerprint on the Saturn finger is likely to perform some kind of skilled manual work, whether or not it comprises the main career. If it is the only arch print on the hand, manual work at some stage of the person's life is almost a certainty. Two of the cleaning women had previously done office work but preferred their present career.

A single arch print on the ring finger will indicate that the person will probably enjoy a craft-oriented hobby. It could be pottery, weaving, sculpture, or a similar art form. Often this skill can earn the person money and may even evolve into a full-time career.

Solitary arches are virtually never found on the Mercury finger and seldom on the thumb. Arches would normally be on those digits only when there are arches elsewhere. It is important to remember that manual workers need not have arch fingerprints. While you will commonly find them among such workers, there are also many bricklayers, mechanics, and cabinet-makers without a single arch on their fingers. In these cases, other features will be present in the hand which will point to the type of work their owner is likely to select. Loop fingerprints are common and can turn up anywhere. What is uncommon among manual workers are the 'high loops', as seen in Figure 6.4. Such loops indicate idealism, and a tendency to aim for higher things. Ordinary loops should be regarded as neutral: a worker with loops could be good, bad or indifferent on the job. Check other aspects of the hand for a more accurate analysis.

L   R

Figure 6.4: High loop (L) as compared with normal loop (R).

Whorl fingerprints indicate concentration, thoughtfulness and a tendency to be self-contained. If found on the hands of a manual worker, the individual would tend to be highly skilled at his or her work. The ability to concentrate leads to the development of skill. Artists of all types are inclined to have whorls on their fingertips, and you may find a particularly gifted plasterer, house painter or glazier with this type of fingerprint pattern. Remember that whorls have no special link to manual skills, but workers with this type of print are likely to be good at their jobs.

The print seen in Figure 6.5 is a superb specimen of a skilled worker with arch fingerprints. It belongs to John Kirslis, a highly talented American jeweller who designed for the television series *Dynasty*. This is a very large hand with the long fingers typical of a jeweller. Arch fingerprints can be found on the Jupiter, Saturn and Mercury fingers, while the loop on the Apollo finger is nearly of the arch type. If you look carefully at the mount of Luna, the seat of the imagination, you will see that

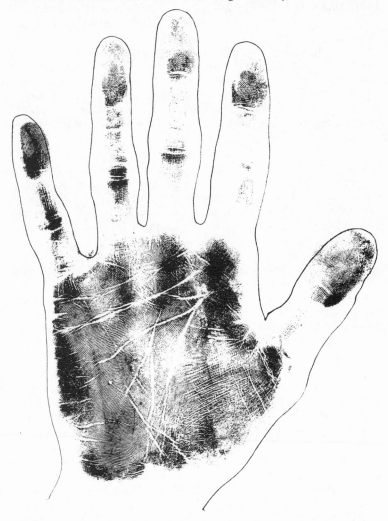

Figure 6.5: Hand print of a skilled worker showing arch fingerprints.

the entire area is covered with thick, swirling skin ridges. Although this is not a fully-fledged whorl pattern, it certainly lends great strength to the influence of the Luna mount.

Apart from the fingerprints, there are other structural features which occur in most able or practical hands. The skin texture on the palm will be firm, and the ridges of the skin tend to be more coarse than in mentally-oriented hands. The lines are never thin and spidery, but tend to be deep, clear, and firmly-formed. For the most part, the palm will be fairly broad, and will be square or rectangular. The life line is usually deep and will tend to curve outwards into the palm. It may be short but will still be strong.

The fingers on the able hand are never thin and tapering, but are always strong and substantial. Their tips can be square, spatulate or round, but they are never pointed. Spatulate finger-tips are often found on outdoor workers or on those whose job involves much physical activity. Construction workers, bricklayers and carpenters may have them. Manual workers with square-tipped fingers would tend to be very organized, and would have a talent to work well with calculations and measurements. Car mechanics are inclined to have squarish fingertips, as are many fitters and turners. The occasional carpenter will have square-tipped fingers if he is methodical and accurate in his job. It is rare to find much space between the fingers of people with able hands, as these folk are seldom daring and adventurous.

Plumbers have no specific features in their hands although they are sometimes shaped in an unusual way. The fingertips tend to be shapeless and the fingers themselves may be short and roughly formed. The simplest description of a plumber's hands is that they lack refinement. It is not the result of the physical labour involved, but rather that plumbing is one of the least pleasant jobs in the building trade. There is a lot of banging and thumping, getting into tight and awkward places, and 'mucking about' in general. The typical plumber puts up with all these problems, which would probably daunt other manual workers. The plumber is unlikely to be a precise, neat or fussy individual, and it is probable that his hands have a rough-and-ready appearance to match the rough-and-ready personality. This does not imply that plumbing is not a skilled trade, because it is. Yet it tends to attract a certain type of worker who can cope with the difficulties involved.

By contrast, plasterers, locksmiths and electricians tend to have longer fingers and their hands would probably be more gracefully-formed. Electricians particularly would be long-fingered, because their career entails concentrating on small details and in making precise connections. The hands and fingers may be of any shape, but the length of the fingers would show attention to detail.

Some manual work requires even greater concentration. The watchmaker and the jeweller are obvious examples, and makers of optical equipment such as eyeglass lenses can join this group as well. These people invariably have large hands in proportion to their body size. It is amazing to watch them work as their big hands perform the most delicate tasks. If a person is so inclined, watchmaking or jewellery making is a good career choice. A surgeon with large hands would be very competent at microsurgery. Mentally-inclined people who focus on details – such as editors and proofreaders – would tend to be large-

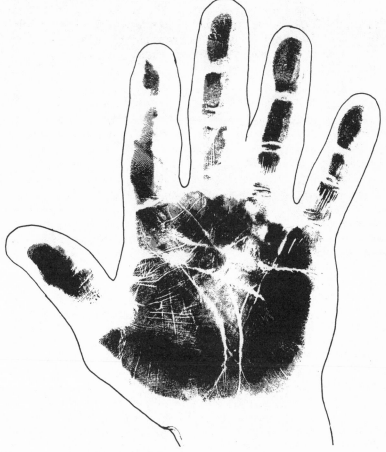

Figure 6.6: An athletic earth hand.

handed as well. The jeweller's hand shown in Figure 6.5 is at least twenty per cent larger than normal.

However, factory workers who assemble tiny items are not as likely to have large hands, because many usually are required to perform whatever tasks are asked of them. Chances are good that you will find many large hands in a factory, but there will also be many that are not!

Finally, earth hands can often be found on athletes, particularly those who are involved in active, agressive sports. Practical, earthy hands could be found on many professional boxers, wrestlers, football players and rugby players. The print shown in Figure 6.6 is a good example of such a hand. One look at the strong life line will tell you that it belongs to an extremely athletic person with an abundance of physical energy. Notice the way the fate line curves around the life line to give it extra strength. The hand belongs to the legendary hockey player Bobby Hull. Of additional interest is his straight, businesslike head line. After retiring from professional hockey, Mr. Hull took up a successful business career.

Chapter 7

CREATIVE HANDS

Creativity comes in many forms, and there is room to be creative in almost every job. We have met creative cooks, creative builders, creative announcers and creative home-makers. In this chapter, we propose to restrict the field somewhat by examining only those hands whose owners are creative in the artistic sense. They include painters, designers, artists and others who create beauty around themselves.

There is no *specific* artistic hand, but the ring or Apollo finger is most definitely associated with artistic matters. As mentioned earlier, this finger is named after Apollo, the Sun God, patron of the arts in Greek mythology. Generally speaking, long Apollo fingers are common among artists, and will be discussed in detail later on. However, a *whorl fingerprint* on Apollo is a far more important indicator of artistic ability than length alone. Although we certainly can find artists who do not have a whorl pattern on their Apollo fingertip, you will never meet anyone with a whorl on Apollo (Figure 7.1) who does not have some kind of artistic talent.

This talent can manifest in many ways. Some non-professional people with a whorl on the ring finger may enjoy painting or sketching as a hobby, or may have a talent for designing their own clothes. Individuals with the whorl pattern often excel in the fashion and beauty scene, and may even create their own product lines. Nearly all who have this sign possess a strong sense of colour. They show style in the way they dress and in the way they decorate their homes.

The whorl on Apollo is always a sign of some sort of artistic capacity, and among professional artists, nearly eighty per cent have this mark. While it is possible to be talented artistically

Figure 7.1: Whorl fingerprint pattern.

without the presence of a whorl on the Apollo finger, having a whorl on your fingertip is a good mark to have!

The whorl is at its strongest when no other finger bears a whorl print. In this case, the artistic talent will be clear and obvious. When other fingers have the whorl pattern, the owner may deny that he or she has a talent for drawing or painting. However, he or she would probably admit to some interest in designing or decorating, or, failing that, to building or making things which are beautiful. One example of this was a professional tree surgeon who had several whorls on his hands. He was a simple man and claimed to have no artistic ability whatsoever. In addition to tree cutting and rehabilitation, much of his work consisted of trimming trees in people's yards. When pressed, he admitted that he had won an award for the artistic manner in which he could trim trees and hedges into whatever fantastic form the owner might desire!

Long ring fingers reach more than two-thirds of the way up the top joint of the middle or Saturn finger. Often this will make it longer than the index or Jupiter finger. However, don't use the latter as a guide since the Jupiter finger may be longer or shorter than average. Generally speaking, a long ring finger is associated with an interest in the arts, including music and theatre as well as the visual arts. Unfortunately, it can also be an indication of a gambler, and there is no easy way to determine which interpretation is correct. Some people who are very interested in spiritual matters can have a long Apollo finger as well.

In ancient times, Apollo ruled over fame, wealth, the arts, and what we would now call 'the humanities'. For an astrologer, all these aspects are associated with the influence of the Sun. Since long Apollo fingers can be linked to these matters as well, the gambler, the artist, the actor and the yogi may all possess them. Of course, if the fingertip features a whorl pattern, the person will be an artist of some kind. However, if no whorl is present, you need to examine other aspects of the hand in order to make an accurate analysis. For example, intellectuals and people dedicated to the service of humanity can have both the ring and little fingers longer than average.

We have found very few artists with knotty fingers. The majority have fingers which are very smooth, revealing intuition and emotion. Knotty fingers go with a logical mind which loves to reason, debate, analyse and investigate. Smooth-fingered individuals work by intuition. The smoother the fingers, the more the owner will depend on feelings, instinct and intuition to move through life.

There is no reason why a logical thinker should not be artistic, but in practice this seldom occurs. Hence, smooth fingers seem to predominate among serious artists. Perhaps the link between intuitive thinking, artistic ability and smooth fingers indicates a dominance of the right hemisphere of the brain. It is also possible that other physiological influences are at work, since some children have knotty fingers while others never develop them, even into old age.

This smoothness can extend throughout the entire hand. If the hand is smooth, soft and tapering, it corresponds to what Captain D'Arpentigny named 'the artistic hand', as seen in Figure 7.2. He noted that many artists had particularly smooth hands, often with a velvety-textured skin. The palms of these hands were fleshy while the fingers tended to be long and tapering to conic tips. In the latter part of the twentieth century, the 'pure' conic or artistic hand is rarely seen. This is one of the reasons why experienced palmists do not totally rely on D'Arpentigny's system of classifying hands today.

In our studies, we have observed a few fine specimens of the conic hand among artists. Several years ago we found a number of female students at the Ontario College of Art in Canada who had what D'Arpentigny would have called 'perfect' artistic hands. Because this hand is by nature more feminine than masculine, it would be expected to predominate among women, although it is still something of a rarity. Those who have this hand are virtually certain to possess at least a moderate degree of artistic talent, although the majority of artists do not have a hand of this rare type. Nevertheless, smooth fingers are a common feature of artists' hands.

Another common feature of the creative person's hand is for the ulnar edge of the palm to be formed in a smooth curve, as seen in Figure 7.3. Traditional palmists call this the *creative curve*, and it is found more often on air hands than any other type. A true creative curve comprises the part of the hand you would

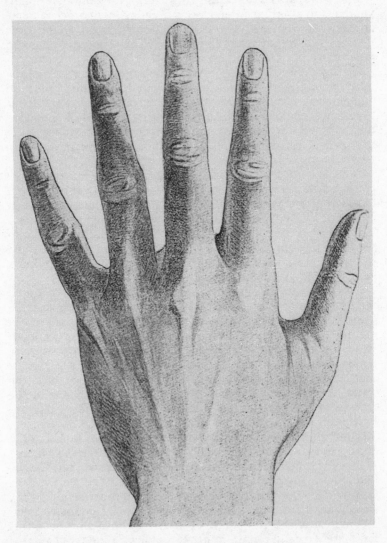

Figure 7.2: 'The artistic hand' after D'Arpentigny.
from The Science of the Hand, trans. by Ed. Heron-Allen (London: Ward, Lock & Co., 1886)

thump against a table with your fist clenched. A bulge at the top (i.e., the mount of Mercury) or the bottom (i.e., the mount of Luna) should be considered as it is: an expanded mount rather than as a genuine creative curve.

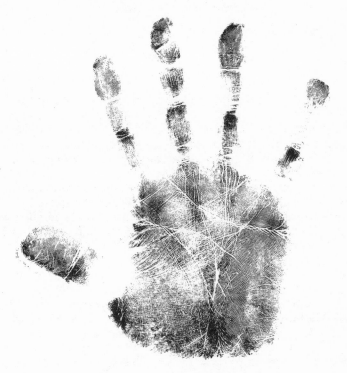

Figure 7.3: Hand featuring The 'creative curve'.

A painter without this formation may well produce competent works of art, but his work would probably not be very original. In contrast, the painter with a creative curve would be more likely to introduce new effects, fresh ideas, and generally more interesting works of art. He or she would tend to experiment more with new media and techniques, and would be more prone to establish a unique personal style. The creative curve is found primarily in artists and writers, and rarely appears in the hands of people who are not involved in these fields.

Artistic people often have *droplets* on the tips of their fingers, as shown in Figure 7.4. A droplet is simply a high, soft padding on the fingertip, and is quite unmistakable once seen. Strictly speaking, the droplets are a sign of sensitivity in general, and artistic sensitivity in particular.

Artistic sensitivity is not necessarily the same thing as artistic *ability*, although the two often go together. People with the droplets love beautiful things: the ballet, fine antiques, and works of art. Any adult who has droplets on their fingertips will

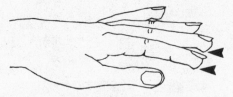

Figure 7.4: Sensitivity droplets or pads.

have a love of art and probably some artistic ability as well. Droplets appear to be common among children, but tend to disappear as the child approaches adulthood. More research is needed to validate this phenomenon, and especially to find out why it occurs.

It is important to remember that even a strong natural talent in art will benefit from formal training. We are acquainted with a young woman who, at the age of twelve, much admired her older sister, who was a talented artist. This child decided to imitate her sister and struggled hard to become a competent artist in her own right. Her air hands indicate good communication skills, she has the droplets on all of her fingers, and her ring finger features a very nice whorl pattern.

At first her work was mediocre, but she persevered until her drawing improved. Five years later, she has become a very accomplished painter, and hopes to pursue a career in the art world. Although her hands reveal more natural skill as a writer, art is far more appealing to her. The three strong 'artistic' features in her hands helped her tremendously, but the five years of determined work and study were the real keys to her success.

Many books on palmistry associate the *line of Apollo* or *Sun line* (Figure 7.5) with artistic endeavours. There is some truth in this, and indeed many successful artists have very well-defined Apollo lines in their hands. However, the Sun line can have other meanings as well. Strong Apollo lines are often found in the hands of wealthy people, and have been linked to fame and living in the public eye. The Sun line can also be an indicator of spiritual awareness or a deep sense of personal fulfilment.

Long Apollo lines are rare. In its most common form, the line consists of a small dash that runs from just above the heart line to slightly below the Apollo or ring finger. Only a small percentage begin lower than the heart line, and rise from the life line or the mount of Luna. Although lines of this type may suggest artistic propensities, they may just as easily reveal the other meanings.

An interesting example of this recently occurred in Andrew's practice in Brisbane. Two young women who possessed strong

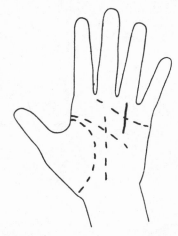

Figure 7.5: Line of Apollo.

Sun lines made appointments for a hand analysis during the same week. They had no connection to each other, but each had a long, strong Apollo line that ran from the base of the palm right up to the mount of Apollo. The first woman was somewhat nondescript with no particularly strong qualities. However, she had married a very wealthy property developer and looked forward to a life of considerable luxury.

The second woman was an artist. She had taught art in secondary schools for ten years and had recently accepted the directorship of an important art gallery.

In a hand which reveals several artistic indications, a good Apollo line would virtually guarantee success in an artistic field. If supporting signs are absent – such as droplets, a whorl on Apollo or the pure conic hand – another interpretation would be called for. Like other lines in the hand, the Sun line is capable of growing longer, particularly after the age of thirty. For this reason, don't lose heart if your Apollo line is absent or short!

Another place to look for creative ability is the mount of Luna. Any skin ridge pattern located in this mount will emphasize the subconscious mind. Since most artists draw their inspiration from the deeper levels of the mind, it is not surprising that many of them have some kind of marking on the Luna mount.

Although all skin ridge patterns in Luna have their own meaning, none are specifically artistic. However, the whorl pattern will show that the individual has the ability to visualize things clearly, an important gift for all artists and designers. A whorl on Luna is relatively rare, but it is found more on the hands of artists than in the general public. A hand print with this whorl

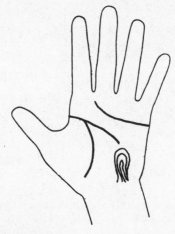

Figure 7.6: Loop of inspiration.

pattern can be found in Figure 12.6.

A loop rising from the base of the hand up onto the mount of Luna is known among palmists as the *loop of inspiration* (Figure 7.6). It is perhaps the rarest of all the loop patterns found in the hand and indicates an ability to frequently experience bursts of inspiration. The people who are fortunate enough to have it report that their minds often seem to burst with ideas, creativity or inspiration coming from some outside source, which is most probably the person's own Higher Self or subconscious mind. Whatever the source, these bursts are always very useful and productive. Of the few people we know of who possess this loop, all are artists who enjoy working in a variety of media and techniques. Although we have not been able to formulate a definite rule, this does suggest that the loop of inspiration is often linked to artistic creativity. Other skin ridge patterns found on the mount of Luna are common among artists as well. The print shown in Figure 7.7 is a typical example.

There are also no rules regarding 'artistic' head lines, heart lines, or fate lines. Some hand analysts suggest that an artistic head line should curve down towards the mount of Luna (betraying imagination), but experience has shown us that this is not necessarily so. Although a drooping head line would indicate that the artist or designer would show a strong imaginative or abstract component in his or her work, it is not a sign of artistic ability *per se*.

The only other line which needs to be considered here is that strange phenomenon, the *simian line*. As mentioned in an earlier chapter, the simian line is a bar-like formation placed across the palm, roughly where the head line would normally be found. The simian line occurs on the hand before the child is born, and is unlikely to change substantially during one's life.

When the simian line exists, the hand has no true head line or heart line, but rather a fusion of both. At times, the simian line forms a clear channel across the hand, while it is also possible for a fragmentary heart or head line to be attached to a simian line in one way or another. These will look like broken pieces associated with the main line, the most common appearing as a fragment of a heart line floating loose above the simian bar. Amateur palmists often consider this to be a girdle of Venus, but it is simply a piece of line left over when the simian pattern was formed. The true girdle of Venus occurs above a normal heart line and is a sign of nervous sensitivity, as seen in Figure 8.3.

People who have simian lines tend to be very intense. They often experience difficulty relaxing, and may have problems relating to others. You can find a good many specimens among people who are apart from the mainstream of society, including members of fringe religions and odd political and social groups. People with simian lines often have strong personalities and possess considerable determination. Despite their difficulties, they are often high achievers.

People with simian lines always have a great deal of restless energy. When found in difficult hands with coarse skin, bent fingers and poor line patterns, destructive or anti-social activity can result. However, for the majority of people, this restless energy can better be released through hard work, or dynamic physical activities like squash or the martial arts.

This energy can also be released through creative channels. The owner of a simian line is always happiest when creating, and those who are physically-oriented love to build things like furniture, machines or houses. Mentally inclined people with this line create books, poems or philosophies. Any person with even a trace of artistic talent plus a simian line will derive great pleasure in painting, drawing or designing. For this reason, the simian line is an important indicator of artistic creativity, as seen by the hand of the noted Colombian painter and sculptor Enrique Grau (Figure 7.7). He also has a whorl on his Apollo finger. The simian line is relatively rare, and can be found in the hands of perhaps one person out of a hundred. However in any group of artists, the chance of finding a simian line is higher than in any random group of people in the street. For a more detailed examination of simian lines, you are referred to *Hand Psychology*.

Architecture is a specialized form of artistic work. It requires several years of university training and considerable mental ability in addition to artistic talent. Architecture seems to appeal

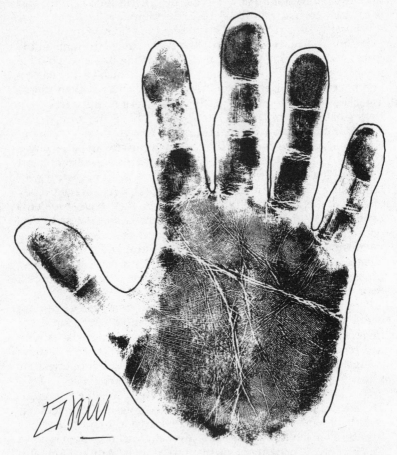

Figure 7.7: Simian line on the hand of the Colombian artist Enrique Grau.

to people of a quiet nature and many of the architects we have met have introvert tendencies in their hands. Usually the hands have a set of fingers held close together, which show no inclination to spread outward. In many cases, the architect's fingers will tend to be long. However they can be of any shape, for this is the only artistic field where the usual rule about smooth fingers does not have to apply. Many architects do have smooth fingers, but sets of developed joints are not unknown among them.

You will find a small number of these people with vigorous, muscular hands, as seen in Figure 7.8. Often they have worked

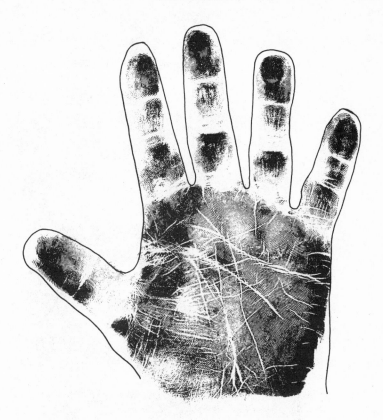

Figure 7.8: Hand print of a young architect and builder.

in the building industry in addition to their architectural career, or they make their living as both architect *and* builder. However, the majority of architects are different. They tend to have narrow hands which, with their long fingers, produce a very sensitive hand shape. Spatulate fingertips are fairly common, even among architects with narrow hands. Architects spend a good deal of time out of doors in addition to endless hours bent over the drawing board.

The architect whose hand print is shown in Figure 7.9 is highly regarded in his profession. He is employed by the government and is often called upon as a consultant on major building projects throughout the country. His hand is noticeably delicate, with the long fingers typical of an architect. He has two arch fingerprints (revealing manual ability), and a single whorl on his ring finger. In his spare time he has done some fine woodwork, as the arch fingerprint would indicate. This man's

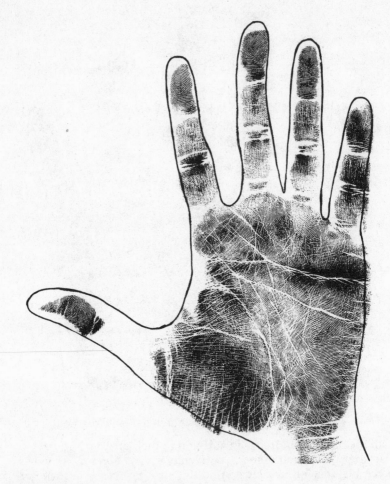

Figure 7.9: Hand print of an architect.

heart line has a very strong branch running to the radial edge of the hand. Technically, this forms a simian line, although the true heart and head lines are present as well.

An architect's hands usually contain no more than one or two artistic signs, and it is difficult to find more. There may be a whorl on the Apollo finger, a simian line, a long ring finger, or a good Apollo line. We have never seen D'Arpentigny's 'artistic hand' on an architect. On the whole, an architect's hand will appear as one belonging either to an intelligent individualist with artistic ability, or to an energetic outdoor person with strong creative talent in his or her hands.

Draftspeople tend to be less exciting than architects, and some of them do not even have artistic signs in their hands. However, this does not mean that they are devoid of creative talent. As explained earlier, it is possible to be an artist without the whorl on Apollo. It is even possible to be an artist without any signs at all, although this is rare. Among draftspeople, this rarity seems to be somewhat more common.

Nearly all draftspeople have squarish fingertips. Indeed, this may be the only clue that the person follows this profession. Certainly a set of squarish tips plus a whorl on the ring finger would make drawing-board work a distinct career possibility. Because all square-tipped people love careful, methodical work, these, along with artistic ability, are the essential features for this type of work. Draftspeople tend to be inhibited folk, and it is common to see their life and head lines tied closely together. Their life and fate lines are often tied together as well. Generally speaking, there are no gaps between the fingers of these people, with the possible exception of the chief draftsperson, who could have a small space between the Jupiter and Saturn fingers. Many members of this profession have one or more arch fingerprints. The arch is a reliable indication of manual skill and a tendency to get stuck in habits or routine.

Turning to the outdoors, we must mention something about landscape designers. There are not many people employed in this field and we have only observed a few of their hands. Those we have examined had certain earthy tendencies in their hands, or at least some indications that they liked to be out of doors. All possessed spatulate or rounded fingertips, and most had practical head lines as well. None possessed a head line with much of a slope. For the most part, the usual artistic features seem to apply to members of this profession.

In contrast, the interior designer's hand usually has a less 'earthy' appearance. Unlike the architect, smooth fingers are more common, and the whorl on Apollo is almost obligatory. Being primarily an indoor person, the interior designer will rarely have spatulate fingertips, and conic or rounded tips will be more commonly found. They are also likely to have strong imaginative or creative signs, like swooping head lines, curving percussions and unusual fingerprints. Unlike architects, they are seldom cool, rational people. You may find a girdle of Venus, outthrust little fingers, an abundance of lines, or other indications of a strong emotional nature.

Among artistic people, the biggest source of employment is commercial art. This includes the production of artwork to illustrate various products, as well as creating jacket designs and illustrations for book publishers. The advertising industry also provides employment for artists, as do magazines and newspapers who require specialists in layout and design.

The hands of commercial artists will, of course, possess many of the same artistic features found in artists in general. However, because commercial work often involves deadlines and requires much personal and professional discipline, aspects like squarish hands, strong thumbs, clear headlines and firm hands would be useful to have if one were to pursue a career in commercial art. Many of these features are found in the hands of Linda James (Figure 7.10), who created the line drawings for this book.

As a profession, creative art is a more difficult field. Although there are plenty of individuals who earn money by selling their

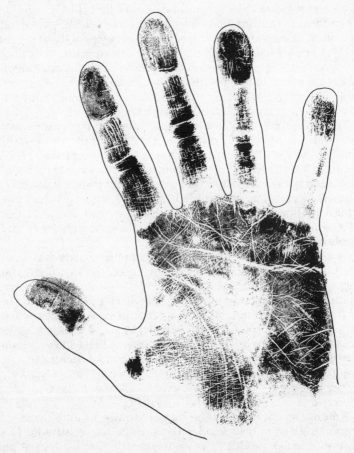

Figure 7.10: Hand print of a commercial artist.

artwork, few are able to support themselves and their families in this way. Even the most successful artists worked at other jobs for years before making a name for themselves and earning enough money to devote themselves full time to their art.

Perhaps a notable exception to this are those who create cartoons, a small but lucrative specialization within the art field. We have found arch fingerprints among cartoonists working in the film industry, and at least one example of a newspaper cartoonist with a full set of arch fingerprints. This invites comparison with the hands of a draftsperson who, as mentioned, often has one or more arches on his or her fingers.

Artistic ability is not particularly rare. In Victorian times, every young lady was taught to draw or paint. Most had the ability to make a go of it, whether through innate talent or through her own efforts. This would suggest that most people have at least rudimentary artistic ability and experience confirms that at least some artistic talent is to be found in a good many people. If you have artistic leanings, we hope that this chapter has provided at least some helpful clues to help you best utilize this talent, whether for your personal pleasure or as a foundation for a satisfying career.

Chapter 8

COMMUNICATING HANDS

The ability to effectively communicate information, ideas and feelings is both a highly useful and important gift. In an information hungry society in which the means of communication – such as print, audio and video – is developing constantly, the demand for qualified writers, teachers, speakers and other communicators is expected to remain high for many years to come.

As hand-readers, writers and lecturers, we not only attempt to communicate our impressions and ideas to others, but meet literally hundreds of people every year who earn their living as professional communicators. Because palmistry is a subject of considerable public curiosity, we are frequently interviewed by media people, including those working in television, radio and the press.

Although many kinds of people are drawn to professions that involve writing, public speaking and the media in general, we have found that the vast majority of those we have seen have *air hands* that are square in the palm with longish fingers. As explained in detail in Chapter 3, air hands are often found on people who love to communicate.

As mentioned earlier, the air hand is the most difficult of the four hand types to identify. New students of palmistry will quickly recognize the earth, water and fire types of hands, yet correctly identifying the air hand will take the most amount of practice. The squarish palm of the air hand is unlike the rectangular palm of the fire or water type, and it is often rounded, which may disguise its shape. However, if you measure the length and breadth of the palm, and if they are the same, the palm can be classified as square. Don't let the roundness fool you.

Once you have determined that the palm is square, you know that it belongs to either an earth hand or an air hand. As discussed in Chapter 6, earth hands have short fingers and lines that are deep, broad and somewhat coarse in appearance. In contrast, air hands have longish fingers with long, thin lines running through the palm. Such obvious features make these two hand types very easy to tell apart.

There are a number of clues to help you determine whether a hand is an air (or 'air-predominant') hand or not. A primary guide is the texture of the lines. The typical air hand has a long heart line with few irregularities. The head line is also long and plain, and the fate and life lines tend to be long as well. All of these lines seem to run directly towards wherever they are heading, with few branches, detours or interruptions. The lines are clear, but are rarely very deep or strong. Earth hand lines are heavy and broad, fire hand lines are sharp and deep, and water hand lines tend to be thin and spidery, with many branches, splits and detours.

Many air hands feature only the main lines with little else on the palm. A smaller proportion of hands have a network of 'nervous' lines which seem to have nothing to do with the four major lines that can be seen underneath the network. In a water hand with a mass of lines, the major lines as well as the subsidiary ones are all intertwined together. In an air hand with nervous lines you observe a major difference: the small, thin and fragmented lines seem to appear in the background, and are unconnected with the life, head, heart and fate lines.

The roundness that is sometimes observed on a square palm can extend to the fingers as well. There is a certain smoothness and curviness in all the joints and in the fingertips. Even square tips on an air hand may appear to have the edges of the square rounded off. Earth and fire hands often have fingers which appear somewhat chunky as well as short, while air hand fingers are more likely to have an elegant appearance.

Any type of fingerprint can be found on the air hand, although loop fingerprints are the most common. For the most part, arch fingerprints are rare on air hands. Composite prints – though uncommon – are more likely to be found on the air hand than on any other hand type. Whorls are sometimes found as well. Loop fingerprints on an air hand tend to be well-formed and often high. Fred Gettings called them 'rich loops': an apt description.

Let us begin our analysis of specific professions with people who choose writing as a career. Among writers, the largest group will be composed of journalists who are employed by newspapers and magazines. Others will work as script-writers for the television and film industries. There are also many who earn an income through writing books and articles on a freelance basis, though not many can make this a full-time job.

The print shown in Figure 8.1 is a good specimen of an air hand. It belongs to David Jones, who started out as a journalist and then went into editing. He is currently Bureau Chief for a major wire service in Manila. His managerial skill is clearly shown by the widely spaced index finger. The Mercury finger is somewhat low-set, but when measured against the Apollo finger it is nearly equal in length.

Creative writers are the easiest to determine from the hands.

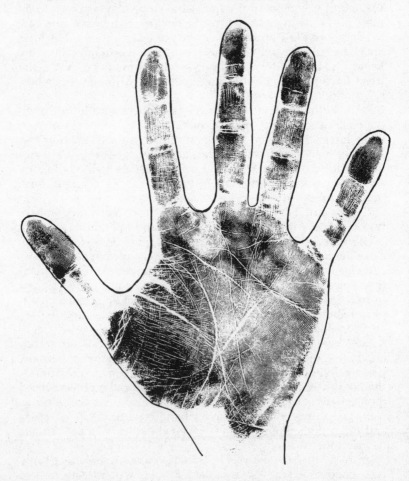

Figure 8.1: Hand print showing a widely spaced index finger.

Every successful writer has an interesting looking Mercury finger, which will probably be long, strong, and well-formed. Because the normal length of the Mercury finger reaches the joint line of the tip of Apollo, a Mercury finger that reaches higher than this can be classified as long. Nearly all good writers have this digit very long indeed, sometimes reaching more than half-way up the tip of its neighbouring finger. Although most Mercury fingers are puny when compared to the other fingers on the hand, the writer's little finger has a healthy strength about it.

In our description of earth hands, we mentioned that they often feature large Mercury fingers, but this is quite different from the 'strong' writer's finger. As a rule, the earth hand would have a heavy little finger, whereas the writer's Mercury finger is long and well formed. It is never clumsy looking.

Occasionally we may come across a writer who will not have a long Mercury finger. In these cases, the finger will be rather knotted with a very square or pointed tip, giving the finger the interesting appearance mentioned above. While you could not determine writing skill from such a finger (as many people have Mercury fingers of normal or below-normal length), you will rarely find a successful writer who has an ordinary looking Mercury finger!

Pointed little fingers on a writer will reveal someone who writes from inspiration. His or her writing tends to flow without effort, and ideas come into the mind seemingly out of thin air. By contrast, a square tip on this finger indicates a writer who works with methodical care. Sentences are hammered out with a good deal of effort, with the writer revising each paragraph a number of times. Authors with square-tipped Mercury fingers are never vague or obscure in their writing, and will make sure that every sentence is clear and conveys exactly the meaning the writer intended.

The head line on a writer's hand will usually be long. Short head lines are never found and average ones are seen only rarely. The majority of head lines will be somewhat curved and will slope down towards the mount of Luna rather than run straight across the palm. Traditionally, the head line should feature two small branches at its end, known as the *writer's fork*. This formation reveals the ability to see two sides of a question and to approach an issue from more than one point of view. This is virtually a requirement for a novelist, because without this multi-dimensional approach the novel's characters would be flat and unconvincing. Even non-fiction writers can have this mark, because several approaches are necessary when performing any type of serious research. The fact that it has been given the name 'writer's fork' is an indication of how commonly it is found on writers' hands.

A hand with a good example of this fork belongs to the Australian writer Susan Drury, as seen in Figure 8.2. The author of over thirty published books on a wide range of subject matter, her hand reveals many of the characteristics found in a competent writer. Her knotted fingers (indicating a love of analysis and detail) are of interest, as is her long Mercury finger.

The writer's fork on the handprint reproduced in Figure 8.3 belongs to a writer of a most interesting type who gained notoriety in the early 1970s. The extremely low-set Mercury finger is a dramatic feature of the hand because it suggests that sexual matters are a keynote in her life. The long, feminine shape of the hand indicates that it belongs to an ultra-feminine person.

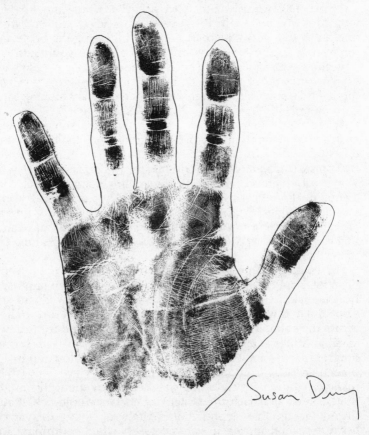

Figure 8.2: Hand print of an established author.

It is the hand of Xaviera Hollander, author of *The Happy Hooker* and other books on sexual matters. In addition to her career in 'the world's oldest profession', she has been a regular columnist for *Penthouse* magazine and managed an exclusive New York brothel for a number of years. Ms. Hollander's long Jupiter finger reveals her ambitious nature and her well-developed managerial skills.

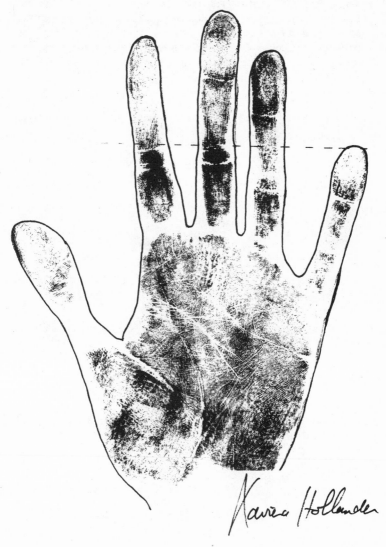

Figure 8.3: Hand print showing the writer's fork.

Head lines which curve to at least some degree towards Luna are almost a necessity for writing, but imaginative writing – as opposed to straight non-fiction – would demand a head line which dips very sharply towards the Luna mount. One such head line can be found on the hand of the American playwright Charles Busch, the creator of the comedy hit *Vampire Lesbians of Sodom* (Figure 8.4), which enjoyed long runs in both New York and London. His writing (which has included plays, television series and movie screenplays) tends to be highly imaginative bordering on the bizarre, with a heavy dose of humour thrown in for good measure. In addition to the long, sloping head line, note the whorl print on Jupiter (a sign of original thinking) and the 'high loops' on the other fingertips.

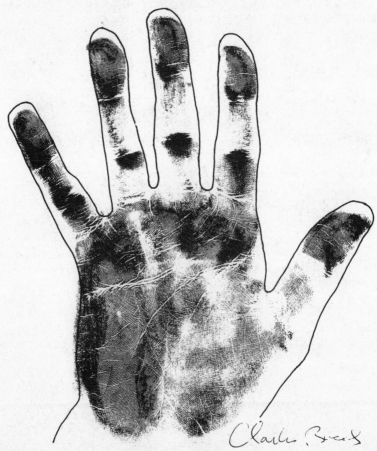

Figure 8.4: Hand print showing long, sloping head line.

Simian lines are found surprisingly often on creative writers. Henry Miller had a simian line in one of his hands, and we have found a number of playwrights who possess them as well. However, we know of no writer with simian lines in both hands, and a single simian line – usually in the left or passive hand – appears to be the rule. As mentioned in the previous chapter, the presence of a simian line reveals inner tension of a psychological type, and creative work is an excellent outlet for it. The person with simian lines in both hands can express this creativity through physical means, while an individual with a simian pattern in the passive hand may well find it through writing.

Writing, of course, need not be limited to the written word. Composers of music are writers as well, though of a different temperament and with different abilities. In many ways, the hands of someone who writes music and the person who writes books will share some basic traits, such as an air hand, a strong Mercury finger, a long head line sloping towards Luna, unusual fingerprint patterns, and perhaps a loop of seriousness, revealing a sober, disciplined approach to work.

However, the hand of a composer should also contain some of the traditional signs of musical ability, particularly 'the angles' described in Chapter 4. Strong line or unusual skin ridge patterns on the mount of Luna would be useful as well, revealing a strong intuition and a fertile imagination.

A good example of a composer's hand is that of the doyen of American composers, Aaron Copland (Figure 8.5). In addition to the many features mentioned above, arch fingerprints can be found on several fingers, perhaps attesting to a love for hard work and his practical, methodical approach to his craft. Note the clear and gently sloping head line and the lines of intuition moving up a prominent mount of Luna. Of special interest are the unusually strong and clear line of Apollo (often related to creative brilliance, fortune and fame) and his very long and prominent Mercury finger. For further information about musical hands, see Chapter 9.

Anyone who has ever visited the inside of a newspaper office knows what an extraordinarily busy place it can be. At first glance, it is a scene of confusion and chaos, with people rushing about, telephones ringing, and voices shouting across the room. A newsroom looks messy regardless of how often it is cleaned. Journalism is no place for someone of a placid disposition who loves peace and quiet in the workplace.

The hands of a journalist do not usually reveal literary tendencies as strongly as the hands of creative writers. The same signs may be present, but they are less obvious to the eye. Many

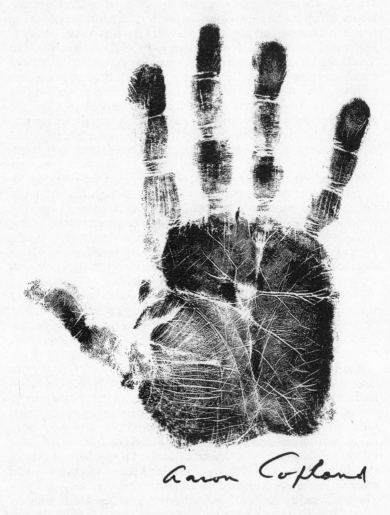

Figure 8.5: Hand print showing strong, clear line of Apollo.

newspaper people have considerable writing skill, but they are often called upon to utilize far more than their writing talent alone, such as interviewing skills, reporting, research and editing, often under the pressure of a deadline. For most journalists, writing is merely one aspect of a complex personality picture. For this reason, their hands often reveal a wide variety of talents and skills. Because the newspaper game requires speed and energy, many journalists tend to have 'busy hands'. For some, this may be reflected by many interesting-looking lines on the palm, a large and well-formed mount of Venus, a hand with firm consistency, or a hand with a strong thumb. Very often the hand will be of the fire type, revealing both energy and intensity.

Newspaper editors tend to have short fingernails, as do many editors who work for magazines and book publishers. Short fingernails that are not the result of nail-biting are an almost certain indicator of the tendency to find fault. People with short nails will delight in pointing out one's mistakes. They notice anything that is wrong and will immediately pounce on it. People with short fingernails tend to be very skeptical, and are always looking for a flaw in an argument or theory. An editor knows instinctively how to simplify a concept and reduce text to the bone. No wonder so many good editors have short fingernails, and that they are often such difficult people to work for! Arch fingerprints often accompany these short nails, adding a practical component to the personality: another good quality for an editor to have. For the most part, senior editors have risen through the ranks in a profession where both a critical faculty and the need to be practical are absolute necessities.

Teachers make up another major group of communicators. Their profession is a very complex and demanding one which utilizes communication as its backbone. It has been said that a good teacher must be a mixture of actor, dictator, super-hero and sage. And indeed, many gifted teachers represent all of these people. However, one does not have to be a superior being in order to teach, and any child will readily tell you that most teachers are not very good ones. While many people can indeed work as teachers, they should envy the select few who have the special traits needed to be a true professional.

The classic indicator in palmistry of a teacher is the so-called *teacher's square*. It is a small square on the mount of Jupiter attached to a vertical line from the top of the life line, and could be likened to a flag. Indeed, the Indian system of palmistry calls it the 'mark of the flag'. The square is a sure indicator of teaching ability, and often its owner will be drawn to a career involving teaching, tutoring or lecturing.

Exactly what comprises a talent for teaching? It includes a delight in explaining things, an ability to share inspiration, and a desire to enable others *how* to think instead of *what* to think. Often the teacher's square is formed around a *ring of Solomon*, the sign of psychological insight. The square is often found along with the *medical stigmata*, which reveals a desire to help others and possible healing ability. The teacher's square is mainly found in the hands of school-teachers, but can also be seen in the hands of teachers of yoga, cooking or crafts. It reveals a person with both a yearning and an ability to share information with others in an interesting and competent way. A young person with this square alone may pursue a degree in teaching at a university, but will not seek out a teaching career unless other features that favour communication are present in the hand as well.

Julius Spier, the eccentric German palmist and author of *The Hands of Children*, observed that female schoolteachers tended to have long index fingers, while male teachers did not. Although this tendency is expected to change as more traditionally 'male-oriented' jobs become open to women around the world, this seems to be true in many countries at the present time. A long Jupiter finger is found on people with a strong ego and the desire to take charge. Many women who choose to enter teaching possess these qualities, and certainly those who make a career of teaching need them. Males with a long first finger would tend to make strong teachers and good disciplinarians, but most men with long index fingers are more likely to take up some other type of profession.

The print shown in Figure 8.6 is that of a former school teacher who is still involved in teaching and lecturing. The teacher's square can be clearly seen on the mount of Jupiter. He has worked at other occupations as well, including those of bookbinder (as indicated by the arch fingerprints) and writer (as seen by the writer's fork at the end of the head line). It is the hand of co-author Andrew Fitzherbert.

The loop of seriousness is common among teachers, as are strong Saturn or destiny lines. Both these features are found on people who follow a stable and responsible career like teaching. As a rule, teachers tend to talk a lot, and they often possess hand features associated with verbal fluency such as long head lines and long, strong Mercury fingers. As can be expected, these characteristics are often found among members of other professions which involve talking, such as announcers, politicians, salespeople and auctioneers.

A long tip on the Mercury finger indicates a skill with words. All sorts of wordsmiths, from poets to crossword puzzle enthusiasts, tend to have this long top joint.

Radio broadcasters often have a special formation on their Mercury fingers. The top joint is longer than average, and also tends to be unusually wide. We are speaking of something more than just a spatulate fingertip — an entire joint that is thicker than either of the two lower joints of the Mercury finger.

This natural thickening of the top joint of Mercury is an in-

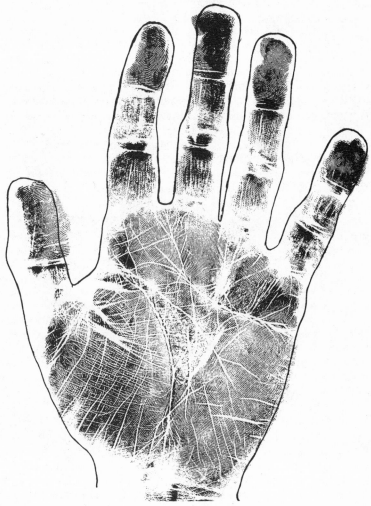

Figure 8.6: Hand print showing the teacher's square on the mount of Jupiter.

fallable sign of talkativeness. Although rare, it is often found on disc jockeys and others who never seem to run out of things to say. You might also find such people in a place like London's Hyde Park or The Domain in Sydney where the 'Speaker's Corner' attracts a wide variety of anarchists, doomsayers and others who lecture from their soap-boxes vying for the attention of the crowds. Sometimes you will find a lone person shouting messages from a street corner. If you have the courage to approach, check his or her hands and you may well find that the top Mercury joint is swollen!

Unusually long head lines often go with being talkative. However for this rule to hold, the hand must reveal a reasonably expressive or intelligent personality. Strictly speaking, a long head line is an indicator of someone who thinks in a thorough, comprehensive manner. Without much intellect, this will manifest as talking slowly in a long-winded and plodding way. A bright person with this head line can talk continually without stopping.

For the most part, radio broadcasters tend to have stable hands. In order to achieve success in broadcasting one must be both hardworking and patient, and only a stable person can manage to do this. The hands of these people are more down-to-earth than you might think when listening to them on the air. The most provocative and interesting radio personality will often have broad, firm hands, with a strong thumb and the fingers held closely together, all features of a stable, conservative person. We have rarely come across one who carried his or her fingers out in an extrovert manner, unless there were hopes of switching careers from radio to television. For all their talkativeness, radio broadcasters are not true extroverts. Their work is often done from a tiny cubicle, either alone or with occasional guests. It is essentially solitary work and few genuine extroverts would want to make a career of it.

Two features in the hand which would be useful for the radio person to have are loop fingerprints and a wide space between the lines of head and heart. As mentioned earlier, loops go with an easy manner, and the ability to get along well with others. The broadcaster must appeal to a wide audience, and when interviewing guests, he or she must appear interested in whatever they have to say. These are skills that come easily to people with loop fingerprints. Individuals with other prints often lack this congenial nature, and may need to work hard to acquire it. A broad space between the heart and head lines is not essential for broadcasting, but it reveals a certain openness in viewing the world. People with this space tend to be tolerant towards different types of people and will be more likely to listen to diverse points of view.

Like radio, television employs many people who are never known to the public, and many people in the television industry never appear on screen. People with air hands love to work in the media, and they can often be found at radio and television stations working as secretaries, production assistants, researchers and programme executives. We have even found them among the camera and technical staff. Air-handed people are attracted to the media environment. They are curious, information-hungry, and love working in the type of exciting and ever-changing environment a television station provides. Television personalities will be discussed in the next chapter dealing primarily with actors and entertainers.

The final group of communicators comprises those who choose a career in advertising. Because this field hires a high proportion of artists and writers, signs of related abilities should be present in the hands of many employees. There is a great variety of jobs available in advertising agencies that offer a wide range of assignments from many different accounts. Those who work in this field need to be flexible and have a generalized approach coupled with a capacity to do things accurately and prepare them on time.

The head line must be clear and well developed. It should be long with a strong bow-shaped curve, revealing a creative, imaginative way of thinking. Interesting skin ridge patterns on the mount of Luna would be useful to have as well. If the head line is straight, it would have to be long and accompanied by other signs of talent in the hand. We would expect to find such signs as a long Apollo finger, a long Mercury finger, whorl fingerprints and a strong, well-shaped thumb. We have rarely seen a poor heart line on a successful advertising person. This may be due to the fact that the job involves a lot of 'rough-and tumble' activity that would not be attractive to a person who is overly sensitive or prone to emotional extremes. People involved in advertising often have an out-thrust Jupiter finger which reveals self-assertion. In a highly competitive field such as advertising, a strong and independent index finger can be very useful, as would a prominent mount (or mounts) of Mars.

At the top of the life line we can sometimes find a small line

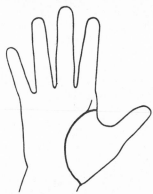

Figure 8.7: Branch from life line moving upwards towards Jupiter.

rising towards the base of the index finger, as seen in Figure 8.7. This is known as the *line of ambition*. If such a line has a square attached to it, it would be called the *teacher's square* and would indicate teaching ability. Without a square, it simply indicates an ambition line whose presence shows a habit of setting goals. It does not mean 'ambition' in the sense of constantly striving to get ahead, although people who have this line undertake projects and aim at succeeding with them. As soon as one project is complete, they immediately look for another. Although you can find this line among members of virtually every profession, the successful advertising person is seldom without it. Advertising is a series of projects, occurring one after another in an endless stream. For this reason, this type of work perfectly suits an individual with the line of ambition.

Chapter 9

ENTERTAINING HANDS

Many of us are fascinated by the life and work of famous entertainers. The excitement, the money and the romance of being a famous actor, singer or musician has led many to pursue a career in the entertainment industry. Whether one dreams of becoming a leading character in a soap-opera or fantasizes about becoming an internationally-known rock star, the desire to work in the public eye as a successful entertainer is, for many, their fondest dream.

Is there anything in the hand that will reveal that someone can become a famous actor? Does the gravel-voiced singer with platinum records have hands like those of an opera star? Is there something in the hand that whispers 'fame!', even from one's early childhood?

Actually, there *are* lines to look for and patterns to recognize in the hands of entertainers. If you have these signs in your own hands, you may be destined for centre stage yourself. However, there is one important factor to keep in mind before dashing off to a career in the field of entertainment: it is very hard work and only a few people ever make it to the top. In addition to natural ability, an entertainer's hand must show persistence, dedication, adaptability, and the capacity for hard work. We also cannot ignore the element of luck, which often plays an important role in the careers of many successful entertainers.

The first place to look is the fate line, which is the vertical line which (in most hands) runs up the middle of the palm. In its purest form, the line begins near the wrist and moves straight towards the middle or Saturn finger (Figure 9.1). However, the majority of fate lines are not as clear-cut as this. They often start a little higher on the palm and usually have various minor

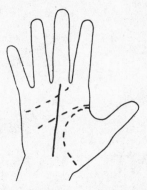

Figure 9.1: Pure form of fate line.

breaks and changes along the way. Most end near the mount of Saturn, although they can also stop short or veer to either side of this mount. All of these variations have a story to tell. Some are typically found among people who work in the entertainment industry.

As mentioned earlier, fate lines which start near the wrist but are joined to the life line reveal an unadventurous personality. This usually – but not always – implies a dull career. We will discuss this further in the following chapter when we examine the hands of accountants and others attracted to quiet, stable careers. However, there is a tradition that men with fate lines tied to their life lines often follow their father's profession.

Fate lines which begin nearer to the centre of the wrist – and thus are separated from the life line – are found on people in almost any career. If the line starts low down at the bottom of the palm, the owner will enter a career early in life, even during the teenage years. Such was the case with the renowned American opera singer Leontyne Price, whose handprint is reproduced in Figure 9.2. Although her fate line is weak at its commencement, it becomes far stronger where she established herself in what became an outstanding career. If the fate line starts an inch or more above the wrist, it suggests a career which began in the mid-twenties.

Fate lines which start further over on the mount of Luna take a slanted path in order to make their way up the Saturn finger. While some palmists believe that this is an indicator of a variety of careers, it has been found primarily on those who enjoy a career in the public eye. People with this pattern simply don't fit into a small office or a backroom job. While they may or may not like to 'show off', they all love attention and need to be with people. Any job which puts them before the public will suit them admirably, while a career which does not will bore them

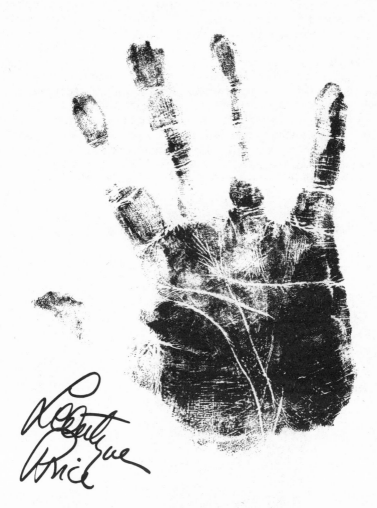

Figure 9.2: Hand print showing fate line starting low.

silly. To conclude that entertainers have this sort of fate line is correct. They often do.

Of course, there are many 'public' jobs outside the entertainment field, such as waiting on tables, teaching, hairdressing, publicity and sales. While the performing arts are always a magnet for anyone with this fate line, other public-oriented careers will attract people with this fate line as well.

The point of origin of such a line can vary from barely on the edge of the mount to near the side of the hand. The further over it gets, the more of a performer the person will be. For example, many successful saleswomen have a line starting on the mount of Luna. They are good at communicating with people. When they have a line commencing deep inside this mount, their sales style will tend to be theatrical, and their personal life hardly less so. Not all actors have fate lines beginning deep in Luna, but it is certainly a common occurrence. When it appears, they are inclined to have this deep and dramatic form of the line.

An excellent example of this line is found in the handprint of a young Australian actress which was taken at the start of her career (Figure 9.3). Her hand has the familiar square palm and long fingers of the air hand, as well as high fingertip loops and long, slender lines. She also has an excellent loop of humour. At

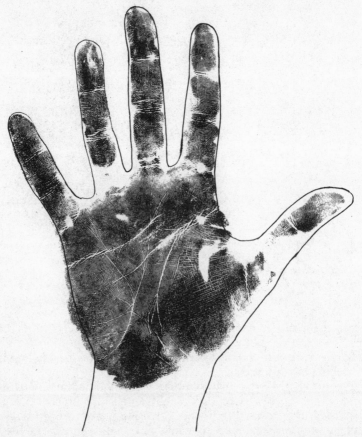

Figure 9.3: Hand print showing an air hand with a loop of humour and several travel lines.

the time the print was taken, she had just completed acting school in Sydney and was off to join a theatrical company in Ireland. From the number of travel lines in her hand, this will be the beginning of many important journeys in her life.

Actors who began as child stars often have fate lines which begin very low down on the mount, although the more common position is a little higher up on the hand. Some entertainers may have two fate lines in their hand. When this happens, the first usually arises from or near the life line while the second (the 'public eye' fate line) comes up from Luna. The first line will often rise only half way up the palm, at which point the second line sweeps in from the side of the hand. This indicates a change from one career to another, and the date can be estimated fairly accurately from the place on the hand where the change takes place. It always indicates a shift from a sedate occupation to one which is more public. If the two fate lines run parallel to each other, the person will follow two careers simultaneously.

We should also examine the top end of the fate line. Most lines stop at the heart line or just above it. As long as the termination is more or less below the Saturn finger, the exact spot is unimportant. Cheiro, the famous Irish palmist of Edwardian days, wrote that a fate line ending at the heart line was indicative of a career thwarted by emotional upheaval. Although a great many fate lines end like this, we have not found that they are necessarily related to emotional trauma.

There is a traditional belief that a fate line which runs right up into the Saturn finger indicates someone whose life is predestined or who is 'a child of fate'. Joseph Ranald, the notorious charlatan who posed as a palmist in the 1930s, claimed that both Hitler and Mussolini had fate lines of this type. Though we question whether Ranald even saw these people, a fate line ending at or near the Saturn finger is more likely to indicate a person whose successful career continues past normal retirement age. In the case of entertainers like Helen Hayes, Sir Charles Laughton, or George Burns, a fate line of this type can be expected.

Two special markings often occur on entertainer's hands. The first is especially common in people involved in radio and television broadcasting, and consists of a patch of lines parallel to the fate line near its upper end. It has been called *The ladder of success* (Figure 9.4) and is found in the hands of people who work their way to the top of a profession over the years. It can occur in the hands of all kinds of professionals, but is most commonly found among broadcasters.

Its presence always indicates a self-made man or woman who has made it to the top through perseverance. Oddly enough,

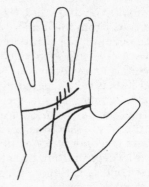

Figure 9.4: The 'ladder of success'.

people who achieve success through their own efforts often feel insecure. In their heart of hearts they know that they achieved their goal not through special talent but steady persistence. They often have a vague fear that one day a brilliant newcomer will topple them, or that a change in management may end their career. These fears are seldom justified, but they seem to accompany the success attained by these particular achievers.

A rare form of the fate line is for it to veer past the side of the mount of Saturn so that the line actually ends on the mount of Jupiter under the index finger. For an entertainer, this is an interesting fate line to have, because it indicates that he or she can potentially become totally involved in their career, sometimes to the point of becoming obsessed by it. They tend to love their work and are inevitably good at what they do. Few people have this line, and those who do are tremendously dedicated to their life path. For an entertainer who strives for superstardom, it is a particularly favourable marking to have.

Sometimes you may look at a hand and wonder if you are seeing a fate line running to Jupiter, or merely a branch of the heart line joining up where the fate line ends. In these cases, consider that both interpretations may be correct. It is very possible for one line to serve two functions. For example, a simian line is both the heart and head lines combined. A slanting fate line can quite easily merge into the heart line and, in such a case, a heart line branch can carry it up to the Jupiter finger. We have already mentioned that the fate line can arise out of the life line so that the two may be fused as one for part of their length.

A trident at the top of the fate line (Figure 9.5) is traditionally considered a sign of success, and is often found on the hands of successful entertainers. Two of the features mentioned in the last chapter on communicating hands are also common among performers. One is the air hand, the hand of the communicator.

Figure 9.5: The Trident.

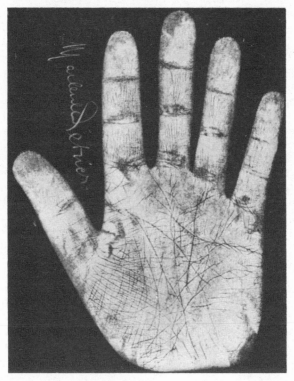

Figure 9.6: Hand print of Marlene Dietrich.

from Hand Und Persönlichkeit by Marianne Raschig. (Hamburg: Gebrüder Enoch Verlag, 1931).

The other is a long Mercury finger, which reveals an ability to relate to others through writing, speaking, singing or dancing. Another interesting mark found on successful performers is a strong Apollo or Sun line. You may recall that this line can indicate fame, money and/or artistic success, depending on the rest of the hand. Fame and money often go together, so it is not surprising that famous performers often have a good Sun line.

One example of a strong Sun line can be found in the hand of the film legend Marlene Dietrich, reproduced in Figure 9.6. In addition to a superb Apollo line, she has a long fate line from Luna and a clear and imaginative head line. Her Jupiter finger is long and strong, as is her thumb, both indicative of a strong personality. The multitude of deep lines in her hand show a great deal of nervous energy. The Mercury finger is very long, though somewhat low-set, indicating unresolved emotional difficulties dating from her childhood years.

The most favourable position for the Apollo line is when it rises out of the fate line. The traditional meaning for this is 'fame arising from the career'. Mary Pickford, the silent film star whose handprint is reproduced in Figure 9.7, had a line of this sort. She was very interested in palmistry and wrote to Cheiro explaining that she had struggled for years on the stage before finding fame in films. She claimed that the only thing that gave her hope was a diagram in one of Cheiro's books predicting fame at the date where the Sun line begins in the palm. In addition to her Sun line rising from the fate line (which originates in the mount of Luna), her fingers are wide-spread in typical extrovert fashion. The open head line confirms her uninhibited approach to life. Ms Pickford's head line is long, as is her little finger, especially the top joint. There is a prominent girdle of Venus above the heart line, which is always a sign of a sensitive and highly strung personality.

It is important to bear in mind that it is very possible to attain fame as an entertainer without having any Apollo line at all. Nevertheless, it is remarkable how many popular actors and singers have a good specimen in their hands, as do many famous artists and millionaires. Remember too that new lines can grow in the hand at almost any time. The Sun line is prone to appear or grow stronger at the time when a person begins to achieve success.

Sometimes the Apollo line could be considered more of a good luck mark rather than a sign of any specific ability. We mentioned at the beginning of this chapter that it helps to have good luck marks to achieve public recognition. What are the others? By far the most interesting sign is what Indian palmistry has named the *mark of the fish*. It consists of a clear 'V' or 'U' shaped

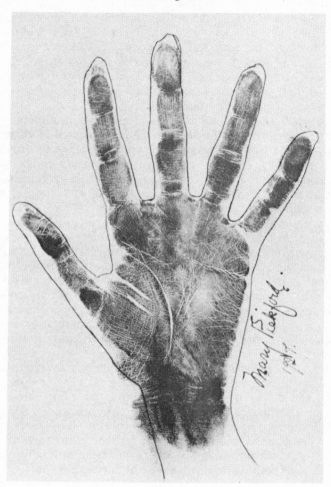

Figure 9.7: Hand print of Mary Pickford.

downward fork, just at the bottom of the line of life. For two good specimens of this mark, see the hand of the journalist (Figure 8.1) and the hand of the former accountant (Figure 10.3). No doubt you are checking your own palm to look for this sign. Many people stare hopefully at some scraggly branch at the bottom of their life line and try to convince themselves that it might be a fish mark. To qualify, however, this marking must be clear, strong and perfectly formed. Nothing less will do.

Indian palmistry evolved some three thousand years ago and has nothing to do with the type of hand analysis outlined in this book. It was purely superstitious and was mainly concerned with the search for special marks in the hands. These had names like 'the flag', 'the bow' and 'the canopy'. K.C. Sen's book, *Hast Samudrika Shastra*, is the best guide to the Indian system we know of. Sen pointed out that he had seen too few of these special marks for them to be considered reliable. However, of these few, the fish was prominent.

Is the fish a sign of good luck, or simply an indicator of overall competence? Those who have it seem to do well at whatever they attempt. Though rarely lucky with lotteries or other games of chance, they tend to succeed in career, marriage and business enterprises. Perhaps the fish is a sign of good judgement, initiative and all-round ability. Or, as the Indians believe, it is an indicator that fate is on your side. Whatever the truth, the fish is a fine and fortunate mark to have on your hands, especially if you aspire to become a successful entertainer.

Some of the older palmistry books suggest that stars in the palm are signs of good fortune, yet we have seldom found this to be true. In fact, stars are often signs of shock or trauma during one's life depending where they are found on the hand. In William G. Benham's classic work, *The Laws of Scientific Hand Reading*, he includes the handprint of a criminal whose death by electrocution was indicated by the star at the end of his head line.

However, a star on the mount of Apollo has always had the reputation for revealing success in the arts or in the entertainment world. You may be lucky enough to have one, but like all marks, a star needs to be independently formed, neat, clear and worth noting. Stars on Apollo are very rare. Even rarer is the presence of stars on the fingertips, just above the fingerprints. We have seen only two specimens of stars above the fingerprints, but both were in the hands of famous people.

Finally, we must mention one of the less common skin ridge patterns, known as the *Raja loop* or the *loop of charisma*. First noted by Beryl Hutchinson in her book *Your Life in Your Hands*, it resembles the loops of seriousness and humour and lies between the index and middle fingers of the hand. For an entertainer or someone else who works in the public eye, it is a very favourable marking to have.

The Raja loop reveals charisma, that rare ability to attract and command attention. Those who have it naturally come to the fore in life, and are prominent in whatever field they enter. Everyone takes notice of the person with a charisma loop. Although these people seldom have any special quality one can put a finger on (such as exceptionally good looks), they always tend to stand out in a crowd. A good proportion of Raja loops

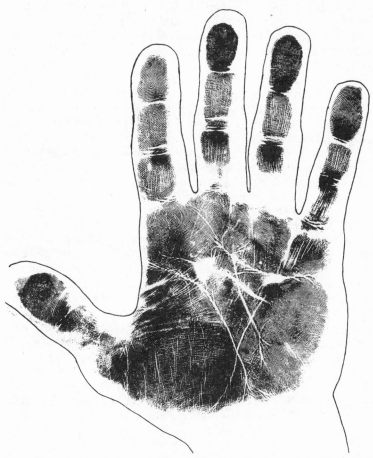

Figure 9.8: Hand prints showing the Raja loop of a former astronaut.

are found among popular entertainers, and especially among disc jockeys who command a loyal following.

A good example of the Raja loop can be found on the hand of former astronaut Buzz Aldrin, the second person to walk on the moon. Though not an entertainer, his hand (shown in Figure 9.8) reveals several traits that are often associated with fame and success. Note the high loops on the Apollo and Mercury fingers and the rare tented arches on Jupiter and Saturn, revealing a person who will reach for the highest goals. A fine specimen of the fish mark can be found as well. Notice the way Aldrin's life line swings out towards Luna and the presence of a massive skin ridge pattern on the Luna mount. We discussed in Chapter 4 how often sailors' hands have features such as this. Aldrin is someone who has sailed further than anyone has gone before.

Virtually all famous people have a large number of small lines on the mount of Venus inside the life line. Lines on this mount often relate to events in life and belong to the fortune-telling side of palmistry, where the hand reader looks for the details of one's personal destiny. Most of the lines – especially those which run parallel to the life line – relate to the important people in one's life. Since famous people are always surrounded by others, you would expect to find many such lines on their Venus mount. Occasionally, you can even date the time when a performer first appears (as well as the time of retirement from show business) simply by a clustering of these lines on a section of the life line. Look for several long lines running parallel to the life line rather than for lines crossing over it.

Other interesting signs are common among specific types of performers. Musicians, singers and dancers tend to have one thing in common, known as the 'angles' of the thumb. As mentioned earlier, these are the bottom joints of the thumb – the first being where it rises from the wrist, and the second where it parts from the palm. In most hands, these joints are barely noticeable, and a pencil outline of the hand will reveal almost no bump at these points. However, when we look at the hands of a born musician, we can see a prominent angle at each joint. Any photograph of John Lennon or Elvis Presley which shows their hands will illustrate these angles nicely. So will a photograph of Rudolf Nureyev's hands, revealing his sense of both rhythm (seen in a developed lower joint) and timing (shown by the upper joint). Nearly all older palmistry books dealt with the angles of the thumb, but many contemporary hand readers seem to be unaware of them. Once you have seen several of these angles – particularly when you compare them with an ordinary hand – you will find them easy to recognize.

Acrobats and dancers often have well-developed angles in their hands. Professional golfers can have the lower joint developed without the upper angle. Beryl Hutchinson observed that comedians often have the upper joint of timing developed, but not the angle of rhythm. Incidentally, contrary to popular belief, many top comedians have a strong loop of seriousness in their hands rather than a loop of humour. This may appear to be the opposite of what we might expect, but comedians like Charlie Chaplin, Lenny Bruce and W.C. Fields were all far from light-hearted people in real life.

Additional musical features may be found in the mount of Venus and possibly the mount of Luna. The Venus mount is usually formed from a rounded pad of muscle and flesh, and can vary from fairly flat to very plump. On a small number of hands the mount is not rounded at all, but is shaped like a sharp ridge running towards the life line. This has been seen by palmists as a sign of 'perfect pitch': the ability to hit a note exactly and to discern when anyone else is even slightly off-key. The formation is rare, and when it does occur, it is more likely to be in the hand of an opera singer than a pop star. It is certainly possible to have a good sense of pitch without this formation, but its presence is seen as an infallible sign that the sense of pitch is perfect.

The respected British palmist, John Lindsay, has put forward a theory that singers may have strong mounts of Luna and Mars Negative (located above Luna) joined together. When this occurs, they form a sort of long, kidney-shaped pad from the wrist to the heart line. Beryl Hutchinson noted that dancers tend to have the Luna mount well-padded just where it leaves the wrist, forming a sort of step from the wrist to the mount itself. We cannot confirm either theory, but both deserve further investigation.

As mentioned earlier, skin ridge patterns on the mount of Venus are associated with the love of music in various forms. Loops which run onto the mount from the edge of the thumb are associated with a love for brass instruments and big band music. A small oval patch of ridges cutting across the rest of the mount (known as 'the bee' and illustrated in Chapter 4) is considered an infallible sign of a love for music from stringed instruments. Although a great many guitarists and violinists may have this mark, remember that it means primarily a *love* of music rather than a talent for playing it. You are as likely to find as many specimens of this formation in the audience at a string recital as among the performers.

Musicians who specialize in piano or organ music usually possess squarish fingertips. Playing the harp tends to flatten out the fingertips and gives them a spatulate appearance. This is a purely physical effect and has no psychological meaning whatever. Drummers often possess very broad hands with the lines deeply etched; these appear similar to the hands of a professional wrestler or masseur. However, the only development most often found on the hands of professional drummers are well-developed angles of the thumb.

The personalities of actors and actresses are of course tremendously varied. As a consequence, there is no single feature to distinguish their hands. However, the standard signs of an entertainer turn up frequently. Air hands abound, and fate lines from Luna are common. Apollo lines are usually found on successful entertainers and the head line is long (which is often associated with talkativeness and a wide range of intellectual in-

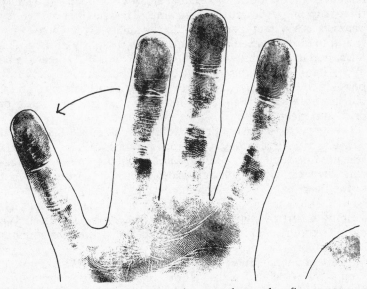

Figure 9.9: Mercury finger carried far apart from other fingers.

terests). Long Mercury fingers – often accompanied by a long top phalange – reveal a love of communication and often talkativeness.

Stage people are seldom mundane or stable. They tend to be psychologically complex and often reveal many conflicting strengths and weaknesses in their hands. In an actor's hand, for example, you may see individual fingers which seem to be too long or too short. There may be various types of kinks or irregularities in the fingers as well.

The Mercury finger especially is linked to the emotional side of the personality. Problems in this area can be easily detected by a little finger which is held out apart from the rest of the hand. If the finger is set low on the hand, it can also be an indicator of emotional difficulties. Look through any film magazine and focus on the Mercury fingers of the stars – if the finger doesn't sport a ring, it will often be carried away from the other fingers (Figure 9.9). If this is the case, it would appear that a good dose of emotional anxiety may well be a motivating force behind the drive to act out psychological problems on the stage or screen. Of course, there are plenty of actors to whom this does not apply. But it cannot be denied that in many cases, creative brilliance in an actor, artist, writer or musician stems from the subconscious desire to explore and work through one's psychological difficulties.

Chapter 10

BUSINESS HANDS

Executive ability and business skills show up very clearly in the hands, as does the lack of them. Two or three good signs recorded in the hands bode very well for both business and financial success. Two or three problematic signs will indicate that the owner may have a difficult time achieving success and financial rewards through a business or executive career.

The primary signs which point to business ability are to be found in the skin ridge patterns of the palm. The *loop of seriousness* (found between the middle and ring fingers) is a good business indicator, while the *loop of humour* (located between the ring and little fingers) is not (Figure 10.1).

Figure 10.1: The loop of seriousness and the loop of humour.

These loops mean much more than merely the ability to make money. They indicate one's basic attitude towards life. A loop of seriousness reveals that a person is serious, dependable and businesslike when dealing with both opportunities and problems. A loop of humour, on the other hand, reveals an essentially optimistic, good-humoured and fun-loving personality.

Approximately eighty-five per cent of human beings have one loop or another, and some people have both loops together on the same hand. The loop of seriousness occurs about twice as frequently as the loop of humour. This means that some sixty per cent of people are basically businesslike, twenty-five per cent are not, and the remaining fifteen per cent are classified as 'indeterminate', either because they have both loops together in the same hand, or no distinguishing loops at all.

The loop of seriousness can vary in size from very small to quite large. The bigger and clearer it is, the more serious-minded the person will be. Loops can vary according to their length, width and the thickness of the ridges that comprise them. Ridge thickness, in fact, can vary throughout the palm. Black people tend to have thicker ridges than white people, and men tend to have thicker ridges than women. At any point in the palm, the ridges can run close together or far apart, and can be thicker, thinner, composed of numerous broken points or formed in clear, unbroken lines. A loop can be so vague that you may have trouble seeing it, or so bold that it seems to jump out of the hand at you. This is something that can be learned only after examining and comparing the skin ridge texture of a good many hands.

Strictly speaking, the loop of seriousness is not primarily a business sign, but it is a reflection of a serious and sober attitude towards life. In practice, this attitude correlates very strongly with business success. Good loops of seriousness are found on highly reliable people. They always arrive at work on time, avoid taking sick days off, carry out their duties well, and pay their debts. They believe very strongly in the work ethic and dislike being unemployed. As students, they work hard, accept responsibility, and get their homework done on time. As parents, they take their parental duties seriously and tend to be very involved in the lives of their children.

It is important not to make the mistake of thinking that a person with a loop of seriousness is a paragon of virtue, because whenever we examine a hand, many other factors need to be taken into account. Criminals have exactly the same proportion of loops of seriousness as do honest citizens. A high proportion of contract killers for organized crime probably have it as well. After all, they are serious people!

Among senior executives, strong loops of seriousness occur in nearly every hand. People who are very ambitious in their career have them too: in fact, it is even more marked among career women than their male counterparts. This may be due to the fact that career women are still in the minority and those who pursue a career as executives or in business administration tend to have strong personalities. Among the sixty per cent of the population who have some sort of loop of seriousness, those with other aspects of strength in their hands are more likely to succeed in a business or executive career. Although people with weaker loops and other hand features may share the same responsible attitudes, they tend to be content with jobs involving less pressure.

The loop of humour has exactly the opposite meaning. The person with this mark tends to be good-humoured. He or she likes working, but enjoys unemployment should it occur. Because they feel that pleasure can be found in everything, why should they pursue a difficult and stressful career? A person with a loop of humour is content with earning just enough to meet basic expenses and is rarely consumed by the desire to earn vast sums of money. For those with a loop of humour, spare time is a great attraction. Good company is more important than a large salary. A pleasant working environment is worth more than being famous or receiving large financial rewards. Owners of these loops tend to laugh and smile a lot. They are popular. They know how to enjoy themselves.

It is very possible for a person with a loop of humour to succeed in business. The obvious careers for them are those where a cheerful, friendly attitude is an asset. In practice, however, you find very few people with a loop of humour in highly-paid jobs. They often prefer to work part-time, and some of them manage to avoid working altogether. Loops of humour are also found on many people who are self-employed.

The self-employed person can work as much or as little as he or she pleases. There is no boss to lay down the rules, and no company to impose its own way of doing things. Furthermore, a self-employed person is usually doing something that he or she genuinely enjoys: for someone with a loop of humour, this is a very important consideration!

An interesting example of this type of person is illustrated by the handprint of the forty-year old owner and managing director of a successful New York publishing company (Figure 10.2). Although her hand reveals a prominent loop of humour, she is a good businesswoman and a confirmed workaholic, as possibly indicated by the rare arch fingerprint on her Mercury finger.

Her book list is highly eclectic in nature, and she will publish only those manuscripts which interest her personally. The desire for fame and fortune are not high priorities. Her office is not typical of most New York publishers: there is a sense of relaxation and fun, and that everyone working there is part of a big family. Her unconventional approach to business can be seen by her widely separated fingers (which all have prominent

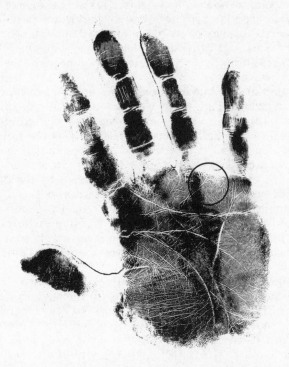

Figure 10.2: Hand print showing prominent loop of humour.

knots), the imaginative head line, and prominent whorl on the mount of Luna. She is interesting, exuberant, and clearly enjoys her work.

The next aspect of the hand to examine for business and executive ability is the Saturn or middle finger. This digit varies little from hand to hand, and is so stable that palmists use it to measure the lengths of the Jupiter and Apollo fingers. These two qualities that are linked to the Saturn finger are *seriousness* and *responsibility*.

On rare occasions, the Saturn finger may appear abnormally long or short. When this happens, business ability may fluctuate accordingly. Long, strong Saturn fingers reveal a love for money and other material things. Their owners work hard for whatever it will bring them. Work and material possessions are their primary interests, and they often become workaholics. In addition, they tend to be far more interested in pursuing a profitable occupation than an enjoyable one, and will accept a higher paying job irrespective of what it entails. A woman with a very long Saturn finger would place more emphasis on her future husband's earning capacity than on his personality. A young person looking for summer employment would pursue the job that pays the most. Of course, we must look at the hand as a whole in order to accurately assess the full personality, but we can be almost certain that for those with long Saturn fingers, materialism will be a driving force in their life.

Short Saturn fingers are even rarer than long ones, and almost never turn up among members of the business community. A man or woman with a short middle finger lacks the basic work instinct, and has little interest in employment, dislikes responsibility, and is often careless about their material environment. In spite of being associated with chronic unemployment due to the desire not to work, this pattern is not linked to criminal behaviour. Owners of abnormally short Saturn fingers can be very law abiding, but they refuse to take life too seriously. Though not necessarily amusing, they often make pleasant company. Their carefree nature makes them easy to get along with.

One of us recently observed a case where the Saturn finger was actually shorter than both Jupiter and Apollo. It belonged to a publisher of several erotic magazines, including a guide to strip shows, escort services and massage parlours in a major city. Although very successful in his career, the publisher considered his work more as a hobby than serious work, and found it amusing that he could earn a good living while enjoying himself.

The relative strength and thickness of the Saturn finger should also be taken into account. While it is rare to have a long Saturn finger, many successful businesspeople tend to have it well-developed. This is another feature that can be recognized only after much experience. The expert hand analyst knows that a finger may well appear strong even though its actual length is normal. If you suspect that this is the case in a hand you are examining, check to see if there are any supporting features.

A well-developed Saturn finger may sometimes be accompanied by other signs of business leanings that are often overlooked by hand readers. For example, anyone wearing a ring on this finger is likely to be very involved in his or her work. This is particularly true if no other rings are worn on the hand. Many believe that wearing a ring is purely a matter of individual choice, but experience shows that wearing rings is often determined by one's underlying psychological preoccupations. In the case of rings on the Saturn finger, it is not uncommon to find that they are usually large and ostentatious. It is almost as though a businessman obsessed with money needs to hang a large, heavy sign proclaiming that fact on his Saturn finger!

Next on our list is the fate line. The simple rule to observe is that the longer and straighter it is, the greater the likelihood that its owner will be grounded in a stable career path. Business and other career-oriented individuals are more than likely to have strong and clear fate lines, because they know what they want out of life and will strive to attain it.

A long, unbroken fate line does not indicate that its owner will have only one career. Someone with such a line may actually change jobs two or three times during life. What he or she will *not* do is change career focus continually. Ten years or more in each job is the normal pattern, and chances are good that each job will be related in some way to the previous one rather than involve a totally different field or type of work. It is common to learn that such a person has indeed followed the same line of work right through life. As mentioned earlier in this book, the fate or Saturn line is an index of psychological stability, and reveals steadiness, a capacity to deal with difficulties, and the ability to stick to things. The stronger the line, the stronger these qualities. In practice, this nearly always works out as a very stable attitude towards employment. Only on rare occasions will you meet someone with a strong fate line who has had many jobs.

Short fate lines may be deficient either at the top or the bottom. They can also be of respectable length but are composed of three or more overlapping sections. Either of these patterns is indicative of a varied career. Fate lines which stop short of the head line do not necessarily correlate with the end to the career in mid-life. However, it is quite common to find a person who has lost interest in work at around thirty-five or forty years of age, which is the time that most psychologists refer to as the 'mid-life crisis'. Others with this type of line may change careers at about this period in life. Fate lines which are short because they begin half-way up the palm indicate several years of unsettled life before getting into a definite career path. Islands, branches and overlapped breaks in the line will often correspond to precise dates of career changes, although the study of these marks belongs more to the fortune-telling side of palmistry and is therefore not dealt with in this book.

Fate lines which begin joined to the life line indicate inhibition in the early years of life. This is a similar pattern to having the head line and life line strongly tied together at their commencement. People who have these signs tend to be cautious, conservative and dislike making changes. Many who have the tied fate line enter a career that is suggested by their parents rather than choose one for which they have a natural aptitude or interest. Often they will enter the family business or take up the same career as a parent. In the former case, the fate line may actually commence inside the life line, which it crosses on the way up towards the middle finger.

The fate line is supposed to end on the mount of Saturn, but actually only a long, straight line will manage to do so. Weaker lines merely head in this direction, and indicate that either the individual loses his or her commitment and focus towards the career, or that work itself may become either part-time or non-existent towards one's later years.

Traditional palmistry teaches that the head line on a business hand should not dip down very much towards the mount of Luna. As mentioned earlier, the horizontal head line indicates a level-headed approach to life, while a drooping head line is associated with imagination. Nowadays, many successful executives and businesspeople possess the imaginative head line, especially those whose work is entrepreneurial in nature or involves a good deal of creative problem-solving.

For the most part, the classic 'business head line' indicates a rather standard, plodding manner of dealing with business matters. A person with this type of line approaches everything from a purely utilitarian point of view, and would ask questions like 'Does this work?', 'How much it is worth?' and 'What use is it?'. There is nothing creative or imaginative about this way of looking at things. It certainly might help a person to achieve security in the business world, but is not the best way to get ahead in life. A person with this type of head line is unlikely to be poor, but is also not likely to become wealthy.

Most fingertips on business hands are square, with the rest being rounded. Spatulate and pointed tips are rare, although spatulate fingertips are sometimes found on the hands of entrepreneurs and others who like taking risks in a rough-and-tumble business atmosphere. Squarish tips deserve a lot of attention, for they are strongly linked to business and executive professions.

As we mentioned in Chapter 2, square fingertips indicate a love of order and structure. Those who have them like physical tidiness, and are tidy in their thinking as well. They work by method and are rarely happy unless they know exactly how something is supposed to be done. People with squarish fingertips delight in rules. They are punctual. They are accurate. They are very good with figures and measurements. Accounting is high on the list of professions for a square-tipped person. Bookkeeping attracts people with square-tipped fingers as well. Contrary to popular belief, a high proportion of accountants possess long fingers that are completely smooth in addition to their square tips.

This is one of those elementary concepts which has somehow been missed by generations of palmists. The great British hand reader Noel Jaquin, who laid the foundations for much of our twentieth-century palmistry, is believed to have started this mistaken theory about accountants. Jaquin knew that people with knotty fingers liked to reason things out while smooth-fingered people depended mainly on intuitive thinking. From this, he deduced that since accountants are reasoning people, they must have knotty fingers. However, his deduction was wrong. After examining the hands of hundreds of accountants, we found that they tend to have smooth fingers rather than knotty ones, and the sign of their skill lies in their square finger-tips. We have made a point of asking several accountants about this matter, and all of them readily admitted to being intuitive people. Although their profession calls for precision, order and the scrupulous following of prescribed methods, it does not call for analysis and debate which are the special traits of people with knotty fingers. (We will discuss knotty fingers in more detail in the following chapter about scientific hands.) For the moment, why not look at the hands of the next accountant you meet and verify this point for yourself? Bankers often have square fingertips, and senior clerks have them as well. Nine out of ten accountants will have them. The exception would be the accountant who is simply unsuited to the field but whose family pressured him or her into the job. This is the only way such people become accountants!

The print reproduced in Figure 10.3 is an excellent specimen of a business hand. The man commenced his working life as an accountant and followed that profession for several years. While in his thirties he returned to education and entered university as a psychology student. He eventually gained a doctorate in his field. He now is a professor in the university's psychology department, and teaches advanced statistical methods to undergraduates. Of special interest is his loop of seriousness and the marked squareness of the fingertips. These features are typical of an accountant. All his fingers are strong, with the Saturn finger especially so.

In his spare time, this man lectures on comparative religion and esoteric traditions. The long top joint on his little finger is both long and wide, both typical of someone who makes a living by talking. He also has a whorl on the Apollo finger, which is a sign of artistic ability. Painting is a favourite hobby, and the subject is a competent organist as well. People with musical talent and square-tipped fingers tend to gravitate towards playing

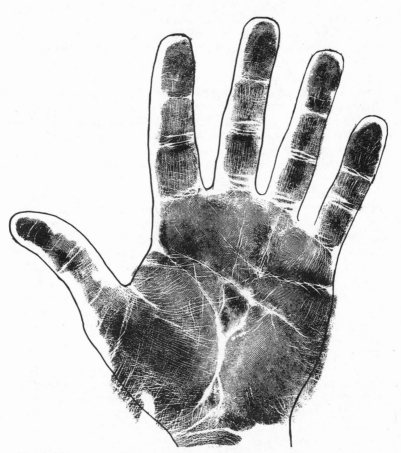

Figure 10.3: An excellent example of a business hand.

keyboard instruments. In the subject's hand, three main features – including the loop of seriousness, the strong fate line and the squarish fingertips – are indicators of business success. The remaining features of the hand, though interesting, are less important concerning our discussion of business hands.

We mentioned earlier that each finger is divided into three sections, called *phalanges*. The top phalange represents the mental world. Intellectuals are inclined to have this section of the finger rather long. The bottom phalange represents earthy qualities, and people who are concerned with the more basic matters of life (such as sex, money and food) often have these phalanges developed. Middle phalanges are related to the world of action, and unusually long middle phalanges on all fingers are commonly found with people who buy and sell things. Shop-keepers are especially prone to having them.

Many businesspeople are conservative, which is usually shown in the hand by fingers that are held close together. In business hands, the middle and ring fingers often appear to be stuck to each other, with the other fingers hardly less so. A minority of businesspeople show more open-minded mental attitudes, which is reflected by the space between their fingers (as shown in Figure 10.3). However, you will rarely find very wide gaps. Unusually wide gaps between fingers indicate a completely open, independent and even radical approach to life which is incompatible with nearly all established business practices today.

The thumb of a successful businessperson or executive can be of almost any type. They follow the usual rule that successful and important people almost always have strong thumbs, while lower and middle-level businesspeople and administrators usually have less impressive thumbs. When examining a thumb, one aspect to examine is the flexibility of the top joint. It should have a small degree of flexibility or, failing that, none at all. If this joint is highly flexible and bends back easily, it is a sign of a happy-go-lucky personality which finds it difficult to stand up to obstacles, problems and other contrary influences. Such people are full of great plans, but rarely achieve much. They are unlikely to do well in business.

Once you have determined that a hand shows business potential, the next thing to look for are signs of leadership. Is the person able to lead and inspire others? Will he or she rise high in life, or is this someone who will probably remain low on the corporate ladder? These can all be determined by observing the Jupiter or index finger.

The Jupiter finger is a symbol of the Self. It shows how we see ourselves, how self-assured we are, and how much we project ourselves into the world. Long index fingers are a sign of self-confidence, while short ones indicate the lack of it. The normal length of this finger is two-thirds of the way up the top joint of the Saturn finger. This indicates a normal amount of ego. People with an index finger of average length tend to see themselves as no better and no worse than anybody else.

A finger which is longer than normal reveals a basically egotistical personality. Egotists are ambitious people and love to rule over others. They strive to reach the top in whatever they are doing, and many people with long Jupiter fingers can be found in high executive positions or are on their way to achieving that goal. Anyone with a long index finger hates being in a subservient position. Young people with these fingers stay in junior positions for only as long as it takes to climb the corporate ladder. Failing that, they leave the company to set up a business of their own.

This pattern appears to be more common with women than with men. United States Army statistics show that long index fingers are twice as common among females than males in this branch of the armed forces. Since at present most senior positions – both in the military and the corporate boardroom – are held by men, a long index finger appears to be not the only sign of leadership, but is certainly a strong indication.

There is a tradition in palmistry that priests and other members of the clergy have long index fingers, and our observations would tend to confirm this. To date, all priests in the Roman church have been male, so this preponderance of long index fingers is an interesting phenomenon. However, the ordination of women in certain Protestant churches, as well as the ordination of female rabbis in the Jewish faith would make for interesting comparative studies for palmists. The index finger is a measure of the Self, including the interest in self-knowledge and self-understanding. For this reason, it also has strong religious connotations.

However, the most noticeable aspect about the Jupiter finger of a leader is not its length, but the way it is held on the hand. The normal position for a leader's Jupiter finger is to be well separated from the middle finger. Sometimes it is so separated that it operates like a different part of the hand. Managers, heads of departments and others in high corporate positions all tend to have this pattern. Politicians often gesture with the index finger alone, a habit made popular by John F. Kennedy.

The way we hold our fingers is not innate, but develops at whatever point in life we learn to 'take charge'. A widely separated Jupiter finger is a sign of decision-making ability. You will rarely see a teenager with this, but the Jupiter finger can appear very independent by the time a person reaches his or her early twenties. Many self-employed people have a Jupiter finger that is widely separated from Saturn, and if you find this pattern with a loop of humour, you can be almost certain that the person you are examining is (or hopes to be) self-employed.

The separated Jupiter finger should not be confused with one which is actually stuck out, as though it were a type of flag. This abnormal jutting out of this finger is a sign of exhibitionism and the constant desire to attract attention. The 'manager's sign' is simply a distinct gap between the index and middle fingers, and is primarily an indication of initiative, the talent to see what needs to be done, and the ability to do it.

Short index fingers are occasionally found on leaders as well.

When this occurs, the index finger is almost always held firmly away from others. This is a sign that a fundamentally shy person has made strenuous efforts to overcome his or her shyness. In some cases, the person may have a genuine inferiority complex masked by a total determination to succeed in life. In others, the person may have begun life with a low self-image and decided to overcome it by simply striving twice as hard as everyone else. This appears to be largely a male phenomenon, and we have rarely seen women suffering from it. Men with this finger configuration may appear to have a chip on their shoulders. They tend to be highly sensitive, and are in need of constant adulation. In many cases, their leadership ability has a false, artificial air about it.

Men with a short and separated index finger are driven by a need to prove their worth to both themselves and to others, and for that reason are not the most easy people to have around. The two most common fields in which to find such men are politics and sales. Dictators are known to have this feature in their hands; Napoleon and Idi Amin are two examples. Used car salesmen and others who specialize in selling products of often questionable value are also known to have this pattern.

Salespeople in general often carry their index fingers sticking out in the same 'notice me' position, wherein the finger is often short and juts out like a flag. Women sales experts often wear a ring on their index fingers. In order to be successful in his or her career, a salesperson would benefit from such aspects as a long Mercury finger (revealing a good ability with words), a slightly curving Mercury finger (indicating astuteness), and loop finger prints, which is an indicator of good social skills. A fate line from the mount of Luna (indicating work with the public) and a loop of charisma would also help them in their work. By themselves, none of these features would necessarily indicate a successful career in sales. The size and positioning of the index finger is the best guide as to whether sales is a suitable field or not.

Within the business world there are innumerable supportive jobs below the rank of manager. Clerks, both male and female, tend to be long-fingered folk with a preponderance of loop fingerprints. The long fingers reveal a capacity to deal patiently with small and repetitive details. As mentioned earlier, loop fingerprints reveal a mild-mannered, easy-going personality. Unless modifying aspects are present in the hand, loop-dominant people are inclined to settle easily into rather uninspiring jobs. Clerks and receptionists often have loop-dominant hands as well.

Secretaries come in all psychological types, so there is no

typical 'secretary's hand'. However, good secretaries always have signs of competence and intelligence in their hands, though few of them show much ambition or leadership potential. Presumably this is why they remain secretaries.

From a palmist's point of view, receptionists tend to have more interesting hands. Their palms tend to be full of lively lines and the hands themselves reflect a basically friendly, outgoing nature. Open head lines and widely-spread fingers are common among receptionists, as are fate lines which begin in the mount of Luna.

Like receptionists, switchboard operators have busy hands that are often of the fire type. Their work moves at a frantic pace and requires a quick and active mind.

This completes our survey of business hands. The business world absorbs a large proportion of all workers, and with the aid of the guidelines given here one can quickly gauge where any hand belongs. The exceptions will be those hands which are simply not businesslike, and the person's hand should be studied in the light of one of the other chapters in this section.

Chapter 11

SCIENTIFIC HANDS

Science and technology are the foundations of the future. The twentieth century has been the Age of Science, and there is little doubt that the next century will also be dominated by scientific progress. Each generation of science builds on the one before it, and the complexity of our world increases each time a scientific discovery is made. Ninety per cent of all scientists who have ever lived are alive today.

The need for scientists is ever increasing, as is the demand for skilled technicians. For this reason, we must be able to determine who is best suited for scientific studies and who is not. In addition, we need to understand the essential differences between the mental skills of a biologist, for example, and those of a physicist, an engineer, and a computer programmer. In this chapter, we will examine a number of scientific careers and how they are reflected in the hands.

The most common feature of scientific hands is *knotty fingers*, which indicate a love for analysis and detail. Some scientists – such as astronomers and physicists – are nearly all knotty-fingered, while others – including biologists and engineers – will have this feature less frequently. Among all branches of science, the proportion of knotty fingers is much higher than in any other group.

Every finger has three sections, called *phalanges*, with a joint at the base of each section. The basal joints (the knuckles) have no known meaning in palmistry, but the other joints are of considerable importance. In most hands they are little developed and the finger is quite smooth. It will appear rather fleshy and the sides of the finger will be straight. Occasionally, the finger will be totally smooth, so that if you ran a pencil around the

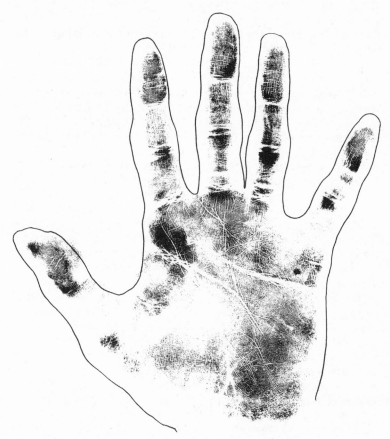

Figure 11.1: Hand print showing knotty fingers.

finger, the outline formed would reveal no joints at all.

On some hands there is a slight bulge at the lower joint. This is the most common form of the finger, which is neither completely smooth nor noticeably knotty. On a few hands, all the joints will be very prominent indeed, as seen by the knotty fingers in Figure 11.1.

Two main types of knotty fingers can be distinguished. Earth and fire hands, with their short fingers, sometimes have this knotty appearance. In these cases, the fingers appear to be strong. The knotting is most pronounced at the lower joint and the fingers have a broad appearance because of these prominent joints. Water hands, with their long fingers, can also possess knots. The fingers will appear to be thin since the phalanges themselves are usually 'pinched-in'. This exaggerates the bulge of the joints. Knots will have the same meaning irrespective of which type of hand they are found on.

Knotty fingers indicate an analytical mind, and people who have them love to argue, reason and investigate. D'Arpentigny first observed this, and named the long hand with knotty fingers 'the philosophical type'. It is true that philosophers often have knotty fingers, and anyone with this hand shape will be prone to philosophize. People with knotty fingers often ask questions such as: 'How does it work?', 'What is it for?', 'Why is it done this way?', 'Is there another way to do this?', 'What does it mean?', 'Is it true?'.

Knotty-fingered people never do anything without a reason. Like anyone else, they make mistakes, but whatever they do they will have a good reason (or rationalization) for doing it. They love to explain things whether others want to listen or not. Their speech is often filled with phrases beginning with 'Because...', 'For that reason...', and 'Therefore...'. People with prominent finger joints tend to argue over anything. They do not mean to be nasty or intimidating, and if they are accused of being argumentative they will often feel hurt. If we could look inside the minds of knotty-fingered people, we would almost certainly find them arguing with themselves! They examine, they test, they investigate and they love to discuss.

Obviously, people with these personality traits are well suited for a job that requires an analytical mind. They also enjoy spare-time activities which demand the same mental processes. Most of them play games like chess. Many belonged to the school debating team as youngsters. While away at university they tend to find a few special friends with whom they can sit all night arguing things out. They enjoy puzzles which challenge both their intellect and spacial abilities. They enjoy doing research and investigation.

Individuals with knotty fingers are neither more nor less intelligent than anyone else, but they tend to make good use of whatever mental ability they happen to have been born with. Others might refer to them as 'brainy', though a better term would be 'thoughtful'.

Knotty fingers are just as common among women as men, an important point in view of the widely-held myth that women are intuitive and men are rational. Truly rational people can be found in either sex, and in any case, being rational is not the same as being wise. Nor does it mean that the person will always be correct. Interestingly, people with prominent finger joints may well have some intuition or extra-sensory perception, but they rarely trust it. They invariably cross-check any hunches they have and prefer to rely upon their rational mind rather than intuition.

Old books on palmistry named the joint of the nail phalange the 'knot of mental order', while the joint at the bottom of the second phalange was called the 'knot of material order'. The value of these terms is debatable. A hand with only the lower knots developed seems to have much the same meaning as one with both sets of knots. In addition, it is extremely rare to find the top knot developed without having the lower one developed as well. Both knots apply primarily to the mental world. Indeed, knotty-fingered people are not known for their organizing ability or their orderly handling of objects. Tidiness (on both psychological and material levels) is a characteristic of square fingertips rather than knotty fingers.

The upper joint of the finger is seldom very developed in any hand. The only times we have observed it is in water hands of the philosophical type, which are long and bony in appearance. It is true that such people are often more interested in intellectual pursuits than in practical daily affairs, but this is shown more by the entire hand than by the prominent upper knot in the fingers alone.

Science has various divisions, and not all of them attract knotty-fingered people to the same extent. Astronomers appear to have knotty fingers, and of those we've observed, not one has been without prominent knots. Confirmation of this finding came from a television documentary dealing with the 1987 supernova. The broadcast featured several astronomers from various countries who all earnestly explained the significance of exploding stars. Every one of them gesticulated wildly with their long, knotty fingers, waving them in front of the camera as they struggled to make themselves intelligible to the viewing audience.

Knotty fingers would also be expected to appear in the hands of others who deal with the physical sciences, such as meteorologists, geologists, and physical anthropologists. Physicists who engage in such fields as atomic energy and aerospace make up another knotty-fingered group. However, prominent finger joints among chemists are somewhat less frequent.

The biological sciences do not appear to attract as many knotty-fingered types. We first noticed this trend among young people who majored in biology at the university level. Subsequent examination of the hands of biologists working with both humans and animals has confirmed that knotty fingers are not particularly common. We have no explanation for this. Perhaps individuals with knotty fingers are primarily attracted to mechanical sciences which do not involve the study of living things. Although a biologist may spend much time dealing with cultures and specimens, the initial training deals extensively with living creatures. For the most part, this type of work will not suit the person with knotty fingers, who would prefer to function on a more impersonal level.

There are a few non-scientific fields which also attract individuals with knotted finger joints. Librarians (especially research librarians) often have them. Clerks who specialize in information-gathering or investigation may possess them as well. Knotty fingers tend to predominate among people involved in any kind of research.

All scientific studies require a good level of intelligence, and having knotty fingers will not make a scientist unless he or she has a clear and incisive mind. The intelligence level among humans varies greatly. People with knotty fingers of average or below-average intelligence may be better suited to pursuing science as a hobby rather than submitting themselves to the mental and scholarly demands that a professional scientific career may entail. For this reason, it would be useful to be able to make an estimate of the person's intelligence from the hands. This is not an easy task, since there is no single mark of intelligence in the hands. To determine intelligence, one must assess many factors. The most important factors are rather difficult to describe, and can only be learned through much experience. Nevertheless, we will attempt to describe them in the following paragraphs.

1. Hands of intelligent people often have a good texture to the skin of the palm. The ridge lines of the skin are very clear and evenly spaced, so they print well when the hand is inked for hand printing. The crease lines – such as those of life, head and heart – tend to stand out well against the ridge patterns. This comparison between the texture of the crease lines and the texture of the skin ridges, which can only really be recognized through experience, is often a sign of a high intelligence quotient (IQ).

2. The fingers of intelligent people tend to be well-formed. They have no particular feature except perhaps that they are straight and strong. Whatever the shape, they will have a healthy, lively look. A number of palmists have collected prints of members of MENSA, an organization open only to those with an IQ of 148 and over. No one has found a distinguishing mark on the hands of these people, but their fingers reflect a subtle liveliness. This is perhaps most striking when you have a group of such 'intelligent' hand prints to compare rather than when a hand is seen on its own.

3. The head line will always attract attention. Intelligent head lines are rarely ordinary-looking, although they vary widely

in appearance. One known type is very long but at the same time quite clear. Although length alone is not a definite sign of intelligence, a long line which is conspicuously well-formed certainly can be.

The length of the head line is related primarily to the speed and complexity of the person's thinking rather than to the level of intelligence alone. People with long head lines tend to work in a more complex and thorough manner than those with short head lines. People with short head lines tend to think quickly and incisively. Both types may or may not be very clever. A long head line which is not well-formed will not be an indicator of high intelligence, while a short, clear and well-formed head line probably will be.

Another common feature appearing on the head line is islands. Breaks and other similar defects do not indicate intelligence, but islands can. This idea is in direct conflict with most books on palmistry, but it is worthy of consideration nevertheless. As stated earlier, islands are indeed an indication of weakness as they can reveal problems with mental focus, possible emotional disturbances, and even the danger of a nervous breakdown under severe stress. However, they are rarely found on people who are not of above-average intelligence.

4. Long Mercury fingers often are indicators of a bright mind. They are most often linked to a skill with words, but most clever people have them whether or not they have exceptional writing or speaking ability. These fingers are usually strong and well-formed, and are seen on the hands of many successful businesspeople. However, it should never be concluded that a short Mercury finger is a sign of low intelligence. We have known a number of brilliant individuals who have diminutive Mercury fingers. All had completed university studies with honours. However their emotional lives – especially in regard to relationships – were totally chaotic.

The only exception here is the Earth hand which often features a large, though somewhat clumsy, Mercury finger. Do not attach any special meaning to this sign if it occurs on a crude or earthy hand.

A major clue to high intelligence may be present when both the Mercury and Apollo fingers are long. This is a common phenomenon among medical doctors and other professional people who work in fields involving service to others. These two fingers lie in the ulnar section of the hand where the instinctual and subconscious talents are revealed. We have never seen a case where these two fingers were developed and the owner was not of above-average intelligence.

5. Long thumbs are also a good indication of high intelligence. The length of the thumb relates to staying power and persistence, while the thickness indicates forcefulness. A long slender thumb indicates a person who is rarely aggressive but who never gives up. We have found that this type of thumb is often found on a person with a good brain and any intellectual who is also gentle and mild-mannered is likely to have one. Generally speaking, any thumb which appears longer than one would expect it to be, is liable to be a good indication of a high IQ.

6. Fingerprint patterns that are of the 'high' type are another clue to determining high intelligence in the hand. High loops, for example, are similar to ordinary loops except that each pattern reaches towards the top of the finger rather than looping near the middle of the fingertip, as compared in Figure 11.2. Arch and composite fingerprints can also be formed in this 'high' manner, which bring out the best qualities of the print's psychological aspects. Their owners strive to excel. It is important to remember that these are not signs of high intelligence *per se*, but high fingerprint patterns certainly are more common on the hands of intelligent people.

L   R

Figure 11.2: High loop (L) as compared to regular loop (R).

7. Among males of above-average intelligence, water hands are relatively common. We have already mentioned that the astronomer is most likely to have long, knotted fingers, yet medical doctors can often be long-fingered folk as well. Certainly any male hand of the water type should be carefully studied for other signs, since there's a good chance that the owner is a bright person. This rule does not apply to females and, indeed, there are exceptions to be found among males. However it is often correct when applied to a male hand and is therefore worth watching out for.

8. Triangles formed on the lines of the palm indicate special technical skills. They are prominent in the hands of many people who are in highly-trained occupations, particularly

those of a technical nature. Since triangles are easily formed whenever three lines cross on the palm, you must not be too hasty in detecting them. Ignore anything that appears vague or uncertain, and look only for triangles which are very clearly formed. They can occur anywhere, but triangles often appear to 'hang' off the head line. Intersections between the Apollo and Saturn (fate) lines are another place where triangles can appear. They can also be found between the fate and life lines so that they appear to be attached to one or the other of these lines. Triangles are seldom found alone, and are often formed one inside the other or joined together in some way, as seen in Figure 11.3.

9. Any line which clearly runs from the life line to the head line (but not further) suggests an involvement with advanced study, although there is a chance it could indicate activity of an intellectual type like publishing books or taking up an administrative job. The date of this event can be determined from the life line. Regardless of dating, a line of this type (Figure 11.4) is never found on a hand of someone who is incapable of advanced education. For a good example of a hand with two such lines, refer back to Figure 10.3.

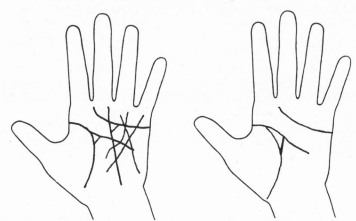

Figure 11.3: Triangles.   *Figure 11.4:* Line from life line to head line.

Of course, intelligence is not confined to scientists, but is merely one of the factors necessary for the scientific education. Knotty fingers and possibly triangles in the palm are perhaps the major clues to a scientific disposition, and there are really no other definite signs to look out for.

It is easier to define what you are *not* likely to find in a scientist's hands. By a process of elimination, an intelligent hand which does not seem to fit any of the other careers may be deduced as belonging to a scientist. These other careers are dealt with throughout this section.

Here is a further list of what *not* to expect in the scientific hand:

1. Head lines which separate from the life line are very rare among scientists. Because a scientist needs some degree of caution and restraint, this would be reflected through the head line joining the life line at their commencement. Head lines which begin above the life line are said to be 'open'. Their owners are inclined to act first and ask questions afterwards. This is not a desirable quality in a scientist.
2. Weaknesses in the hand are very unlikely except in regard to emotions. Bends and irregularities in the fingers, breaks and other flaws in the lines, and disturbances in the skin ridge patterns are all indications of personality problems. While scientists are as liable to emotional difficulties as anyone else, their emotional lives can often be kept separate from the discipline and concentration needed for a scientific career.
3. As can be expected, loops of seriousness are often found in the hands of scientists. It is uncommon to find either a loop of humour or a 'no loops' pattern. This is also the case among most serious businesspeople and is by no means limited to scientists.
4. Short fingers are uncommon except among engineers. Short-fingered people tend to always be in a hurry. They think and act quickly and tend to see things as a whole. It seems that almost each one of the hundred or so engineers we have met possesses either an earth or a fire hand, which are the two types which feature short fingers. Unfortunately we have yet to meet a woman working in engineering to determine whether this holds true for females.

We do have one case of a woman heading an earth-moving company and hers were classic fire hands of a solid, earthy type. This earthy tendency applies to most males with fire hands who are employed as engineers. The skin ridges are inclined to be broad and there may be an arch fingerprint or two as well. Lines tend to be thick. A man with an earth hand who happens to be highly intelligent is very likely to pursue a career in engineering or to enter some kind of related technical field. Indeed, if a palmist badly underestimates the intelligence of someone's hands, there is a good chance the person will be an engineer. We have seen the hand prints of one engineer who was also a skilled violinist. His hands were the perfect earth type, with apparently no clue to the brilliant mind he possessed.

In addition, many engineers' hands possess a special mark. Like the teacher's square and the medical stigmata, it is almost a trademark. The mark of an engineer is a special type of head line that is short, straight and with a gentle downward slope. The shortness is accentuated by the fact that the line does not taper towards its end. While most head lines do thin out, the engineer's line looks as if it has been abruptly cut off half to two-thirds of the way across the hand. If you see one of these head lines on a fire hand, you can be fairly certain that the owner is an engineer of some kind. A hand print of an electronics engineer is shown in Figure 11.5. Though the head line is slightly longer than most, it is clear and does not taper off at the end. Note especially the high loops on the Saturn finger, as well as the

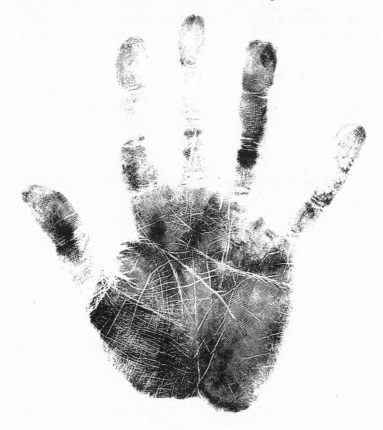

Figure 11.5: Hand print of a highly successful electronics engineer.

strong arch/loop combination on the index finger. Until his death at the age of fifty-two, the subject's career as an engineer was very successful, with over one hundred patents for inventions to his credit.

We have no explanation why an engineer's head line should appear as it does. The qualities of a short head line are well-known, and include a clear, incisive way of thinking and a no-nonsense, 'get-to-the-point' type of mind. If the intelligence is poor and the head line of this type, the rest of the hand would appear inferior. If the hand is impressive and the head line of this type, experience tells us that the owner will most probably be an engineer.

All engineers specialize in a particular area, such as mining, nuclear engineering, mechanical engineering or electronics. If the engineer's field of specialization is very narrow, you may find a single whorl fingerprint on the middle finger, indicating that the person is indeed a specialist. We have seen at least one hydraulic engineer with this pattern and another who worked exclusively at the design and installation of nuclear power stations. Of course, this pattern can occur on the Saturn finger of any specialist and is not limited to the fingers of engineers.

The largest of all scientific fields today is computer technology. Unfortunately, it is impossible to lay down any rules about the hands of people who work with computers. The time is coming when nearly everybody will have at least some contact with these machines. When the modern computer was first developed after World War II, only those very interested in the field were involved. Today, all kinds of people are employed in computer-related work.

Higher-level computer people such as programmers and those working in the design and development of computers have definite features in their hands which reflect their ability and interest. For the most part, they are the same characteristics that distinguished the original computer enthusiasts when the UNIVAC computer came into existence in the 1950s. Eighty per cent are long-fingered folk, and nearly all of the remainder possess classic fire hands with a long palm, short fingers and a predominance of whorl fingerprints. Fire hands are prone to having whorls and fire hands belonging to computer specialists are often totally dominated by them. Whorls are common among long-fingered computer people as well.

A good set of whorls reveals the ability to focus one's attention. Fire hands like to work in busy or high-pressure environments, and the intense mental concentration necessary for computer programming definitely suits the 'whorl mentality'. Long fingers – with or without whorls – are the most common type among computer programmers, researchers and designers. They reveal the capacity to work in a thorough, patient and detailed manner.

These long fingers are often accompanied by a long head line with a pronounced downward curve, which was first noticed among computer specialists of the 1960s. Traditionally, a line of this type is associated with imagination and not scientific thinking, and is the typical head line of the writer of fiction. However, many early computer people had this type of head line. A typical male computer specialist of that era had long hair, read science fiction, and may have believed in flying saucers. Nowadays, the average computer person is nothing like this, although there are

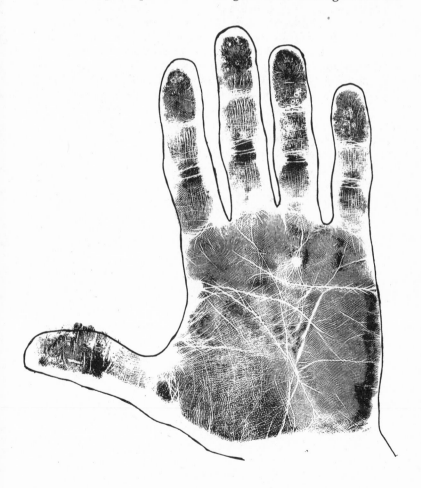

Figure 11.6: Hand print showing strong whorls and knotty fingers.

still a few of this type around. They often are involved in computer design and programming.

The print shown in Figure 11.6 belongs to a computer specialist employed by a major manufacturer of computers and other business machines. The strong whorls, curving head line and knotty fingers are all typical of specialists involved in his field. In addition to his work, this man is a champion chess player and has travelled extensively throughout the world. Although a fire hand, the fingers are somewhat longer than usual. The subject's love of travel is reflected by his life line ending on the mount of Luna. There is also a strong 'poison line' in this hand, which will be discussed in the following chapter.

We would like to conclude our discussion of scientific hands with the reminder that the world is changing rapidly. More jobs than ever before require some level of scientific expertise, and many demand at least a rudimentary knowledge of computers and how to operate them. Youngsters today are taking to machines to an extent that may astonish their parents. For anyone older than thirteen who has no interest in computers, we suggest you reconsider. You may well find yourself left behind in the coming era if you refuse to accept the technological changes that are rapidly taking place around us.

Chapter 12

HEALING HANDS

It is truly said that wealth, fame and success are worthless without the health to enjoy them. Although nearly everyone is interested in health and healing, only some of us will choose health care as a profession. As in other careers, the hands can reveal whether or not we are suited to this particular professional field. Healers of all types – including medical doctors, nurses, massage therapists and naturopaths – have obvious signs in their hands which betray both an interest and an ability in healing the body. So do those who heal the mind, such as psychologists, counsellors and social workers. It is very rare to find anyone working in these careers whose hands do not proclaim that fact. It is equally rare to find someone with these markings who has never worked in some type of healing capacity, whether professionally or as a volunteer.

The most common of these signs is known as the *medical stigmata*. The pattern is also known as *samaritan lines*. It is composed of a small group of vertical lines situated on the mount of Mercury under the little finger (Figure 12.1). Just about everyone who has these lines in this position is likely to work as a healer in some capacity or other, and the hands of natural therapists, dentists, medical doctors, paramedics and social workers reveal this line pattern regularly.

Since this pattern is not particularly rare (samaritan lines are found on perhaps ten to fifteen per cent of all hands), it should be relatively easy to locate and identify. However, to avoid possible confusion, here are a few guidelines towards its proper identification:

1. The medical stigmata must be composed of at least three

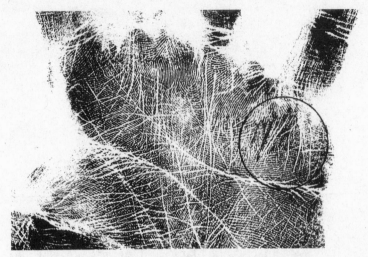

Figure 12.1: Hand print showing medical stigmata.

strokes and probably no more than seven. Don't look at one or two scraggly lines and decide that they must be an embryonic form of the stigmata. Similarly, if there is a dense mass of dozens of lines, this should not be taken as an oversized medical stigmata: the true pattern is always composed of a small, neat patch of vertical lines.

2. If the entire area under all the fingers is covered with small lines, don't focus on those on the mount of Mercury and declare them to be the stigmata. It is a distinct and separate cluster of strokes.

3. One or two palmistry books have suggested that a true medical stigmata must feature a cross-bar joining all the vertical strokes. This is erroneous. There is also no need for all the lines to be the same length as long as they are fairly similar and appear as a set.

The very name – medical stigmata – shows how strongly this marking is linked to the medical profession. Adults with this mark have often dreamed of becoming doctors or nurses when they were children, and many decided to pursue a medical career. Others are drawn to some other kind of medically-oriented work. For some, this may be as simple as taking a first-aid course, or it may manifest as a lifetime devoted to caring for sick relatives regardless of any formal training. They may also be the type of people who friends and relatives automatically consult when they need advice concerning health-related issues or psychological problems. Nine times out of ten, those who possess samaritan lines become engaged in healing at some time in their lives.

A good set of samaritan lines can be found in the hand of Dr Benjamin Spock (Figure 12.2), the famous paediatrician and peace-activist. His palm is long and his fingers are straight and well-formed, suggesting an intelligent, well-balanced human being. His heart line is of the humanitarian type, revealing his capacity for compassion and caring for others.

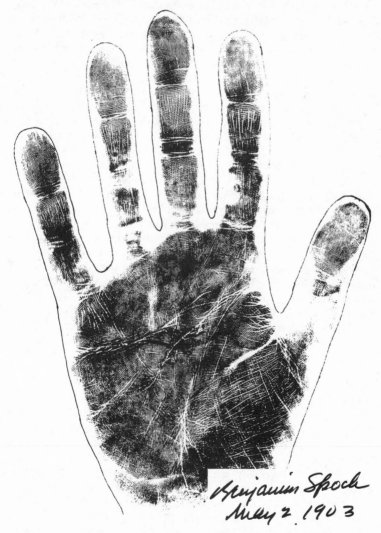

Figure 12.2: Hand print of famous paediatrician Dr Benjamin Spock.

Although the majority of professional healers have a group of samaritan lines in their hands, their presence is by no means universal. Among nurses, the proportion of hands with the stigmata approaches 100 per cent. Among chiropractors, naturopaths and holistic healers, the proportion is nearly as high. Yet among medical doctors, the stigmata is not nearly as common, for reasons we will discuss later on.

On rare occasions you may find this marking in the hands of someone who has no interest in healing. However, you may discover through further investigation that the individual has a history of being forced to perform medically-oriented work against his or her will. For example, we know of one young school-teacher who learned about the stigmata in a palmistry book and scornfully rejected the interpretation as being applicable to himself. Then at twenty years of age he was conscripted into the army and assigned to the medical corps. A crash course in nursing followed, with orders to work in a military hospital. Having completed his service a few years later, he applied to the government to work as a clerk. He was accepted and appointed to the Department of Veterans Affairs, where he spent his time processing medical claims and arranging medical exams for former soldiers. At this point, he had to admit that the medical stigmata certainly applied to his life even though he had no particular interest in medicine or healing.

As mentioned earlier, medical doctors do not possess the stigmata nearly as frequently as members of other helping professions. The reason seems to be that many become doctors for reasons which have little to do with healing people. Although many orthodox physicians are dedicated and selfless individuals, a minority choose a career in medicine primarily for the power, financial rewards and prestige it provides. Some may come from families where it is the accepted tradition to become a doctor. These people may become skilled and efficient healers but they will never have the longing to help and serve others which so often distinguishes those who have the medical stigmata in their hands.

By contrast, practically no one becomes a nurse without a strong interest in the healing arts. Nursing is a difficult and demanding career. The responsibilities of the job are high and the pressures are unrelenting. In many parts of the world, nurses are still grossly underpaid, although the situation is gradually changing. People of all types are attracted to nursing, and you will find all sorts of hands among them. Water hands – a basically feminine hand – are perhaps the most common, simply because the vast majority of nurses are female. However, fire and earth hands occur more frequently among nurses than in a comparable group of females. Nursing is hard work and is far from glamorous, calling for a tremendous amount of physical effort. People with earth or fire hands tend to be better suited for such things. The nurse with water hands who does not shirk from performing these tasks deserves a lot of credit!

In a nurse's hand, the medical stigmata is often the most striking feature. The rest of the hand may have a 'middle-of-the-road' appearance. The fate line is usually strong and the fingers are held quite close together. There may be an absence of any other strong indications and, in such cases, the medical stigmata points strongly to nursing as the right career choice. Nurses are invariably very competent people, and you are not likely to find major weaknesses in their hands.

A high proportion of medical doctors have hands that are longer than average. Sometimes this length occurs on purely water hands, which feature a long palm with long fingers. We pointed out in Chapter 11 that water hands are quite commonly found among men of above-average intelligence, and allopathic physicians are obviously a highly intelligent group. In other cases, the male medical doctor will most likely have a fire hand that will be somewhat larger than the average male fire hand. We have never seen a physician with an earth hand, and seldom see air-handed doctors either.

From our experience, it would appear that all doctors have strong Mercury fingers, and often a prominent Apollo finger as well. This dual feature was mentioned in the previous chapter as a sign of strong intelligence, and is found more often among medical doctors than any other intelligent group. Johan Hjelmborg, the respected Danish palmist, first brought this configuration to our attention. He claims that long Mercury with long Apollo fingers relate to both high intelligence and the desire to be of service to others.

We have also observed a surprising number of simian lines in the hands of medical doctors. In every case, the doctor concerned has been a specialist with many years of advanced medical study to his or her credit. It is probably true that any group of particularly high achievers would show more than the average number of simian lines. This line is not common among those of genius level, but when it does occur, the addition of tenacity and energy to a good intellect makes a formidable combination.

Unfortunately, many medical doctors are disturbingly narrow in their thinking, and those physicians who pioneer new techniques are forever complaining about the conservatism of their fellows. The medical profession has a long history of opposing new ideas in both the prevention and treatment of disease, and this narrow-mindedness can be seen in their hands. Indications of conservatism in the average doctor include a head line that is tied to the line of life, a lack of space between the fingers, and a slight narrowness between the lines of heart and head. Noel Jaquin, the great English palmist, called this space 'the vision metre'. It is measured anywhere between the middle and ring fingers. The wider the space, the more broad-minded the person, as seen by the prints compared in Figure 12.3. As you will see, broad spaces are not very common among medical doctors!

Another formation to look for in a healer's hands is the heart line. This line is an index of one's emotional and sexual nature, so it normally has little to do with career choices. The exception to the rule is the long, straight 'mental' heart line, which is strongly associated with careers in healing and counselling. A heart line of this type ends under the mount of Jupiter at least half-way under the index finger. It may curve up very slightly or droop downwards a bit, but never enough to detract from its basically straight path. It will typically run as straight as though drawn with a ruler (Figure 12.4).

This line, known as the *humanitarian heart line*, is a sign of selfless idealism. Those who have it care about others and often take up a profession involving such caring. In their romantic af-

(narrow space)

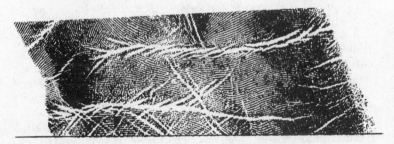

(broad space)

Figure 12.3: Hand prints showing the 'vision metre'.

Figure 12.4: 'Humanitarian' heart line.

fairs, those with this heart line tend to look after their loved ones. They delight in offering care and attention and make devoted spouses and parents. They never tire of supporting and helping anyone they happen to be fond of, and often fall in love with someone in need of special care. People with this line may choose a mate with physical handicaps or other medical problems, or marry someone who is either neurotic or psychologically unstable. Friends will wonder why they remain with a spouse who anyone else whould have left long ago. One glance at this person's heart line can tell why. Who looks after granny when she is bed-ridden? The grandchild with the humanitarian heart line. No wonder this type of heart line is common among healers.

Practitioners of natural therapies tend to be very different in character from conventional doctors. They are drawn to the use of techniques which emphasize a gentle, natural form of healing. A naturopath's or homoeopath's attitude is fundamentally softer than that of most medical doctors or surgeons. It is to be expected that humanitarian heart lines should abound among members in this field.

Social workers also share this softer approach to their profession. If you examine the hands of the staff at your local crisis centres or in those running shelters for the sick or homeless, you will encounter quite a few with this type of heart line. We have both noticed the hands of missionaries working with the poorest people in India, and in most cases, they had prominent humanitarian heart lines. Many of these missionaries were offering medical care as well as uplifting spiritual advice.

We mentioned earlier in this chapter that the medical stigmata has sometimes been called 'samaritan lines'. It is an old name taken from the biblical parable of the Good Samaritan. The name was popular earlier in this century, but is seldom used today despite the fact that social workers with no training sometimes have the mark. It may well be that the stigmata is a sign of caring for others usually in a medical sense, but also through other means. If this is true, there may well be a link between the medical stigmata and the humanitarian heart line.

Psychologists who practise in similar fields to those of the social worker are likely to have this heart line as well. Industrial psychologists, business psychologists and others in less caring occupations usually do not. Psychotherapists as a whole normally possess the 'ring of Solomon', which is a diagonal line running either straight or curved across the mount of Jupiter (Figure 12.5). It reaches from about the start of the head line to a point between the first and second fingers. The ring of Solomon can sometimes be composed of two parallel lines. Strong forms of this line are always long and clear, while weaker lines may be shorter and cover perhaps only half the mount. Some trace of this line is found on one hand in three, but good, strong specimens occur on only perhaps ten per cent of all hands.

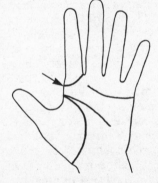

Figure 12.5: Ring of Solomon.

People with this line will be fascinated by human nature. They will take an interest in the lives of their friends and enjoy discussing the friends' problems and difficulties and offer helpful advice. They read books and articles about the mind. They are natural psychologists, and are often referred to as amateur psychologists by friends and acquaintances. It is cer-

tainly an advantage for the professional psychologist to have a
ring of Solomon, and indeed, many do. Lawyers make up
another group who possess this line. The teacher's square, mentioned in Chapter 8, is often formed partially by a ring of
Solomon.

Astrologers and palmists also tend to have this marking, and
some palmistry books have suggested that the ring of Solomon
indicates mastery of the occult sciences. While open to question,
it must be remembered that in days gone by, the astrologers and
palmists were the equivalent of today's psychologists. We feel
that it is more the presence of psychological insight than occult
power which accounts for this mark being found in the hands of
astrologers, palmists, graphologists and others involved in
related fields.

Some early Victorian palmistry books claimed that the ring of
Solomon is formed by a heart line which curls all the way
around the back of the index finger. This is obvious nonsense,
and arose from a misreading of the medieval palmistry texts: an
understandable error considering how much language has
changed since that time. It is an example of the type of erroneous ideas which were abandoned by palmists towards the
beginning of this century.

A similar mistake occurred with the mark known as the *via
lascivia*, which is commonly seen in the hands of naturopaths
and others who work with natural healing methods. The via
lascivia consists of a bar line which slashes across the mount of
Luna (Figure 12.6). In its strongest form, the end curves down to
cut through the bottom of the life line. Both the straight and

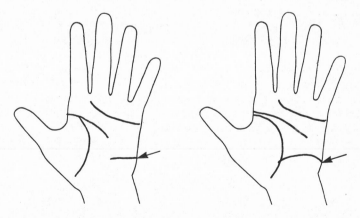

Figure 12.6: The via lascivia, revealing straight (L) and curved (R)
varieties.

curved forms indicate a special sensitivity to drugs, chemicals and other toxic substances.

Old palmistry books described the via lascivia as 'ye sister line to ye hepatica'. The hepatica line is known in modern palmistry as 'the health line', and runs up the palm towards the mount of Mercury under the little finger. Several early French palmists concluded that the via lascivia must run parallel to the health line. While some lines do indeed run parallel to this line, the normal position for the via lascivia is across the mount of Luna.

Members of the London Cheirological Society (which functioned from 1889 to 1940) were the first to notice how frequently the cross line on the mount of Luna appeared. They began to associate the mark with a craving for drugs, and therefore named it 'the line of drugs'. A generation later, the German palmist, Julius Spier, independently discovered the meaning of this line, calling it 'the poison line'. Perhaps the older name is deceiving, for 'lascivia' has nothing to do with the modern word lascivious. It refers to a far older meaning associated with the lust for stimulants and intoxicants rather than sexual lustfulness and lewdness.

People with this 'poison line' react very strongly to all kinds of chemical substances. These include prescribed drugs, chemical additives in food, alcohol, tobacco, and controlled substances like cocaine and marihuana. They also may suffer from allergies to penicillin, bee-stings, pollen (hay fever), and can have adverse reactions to a wide variety of common industrial and household chemicals which make up so much of our modern environment.

Addiction is most often related to elements found in common foodstuffs – such as salt, sugar and caffeine – rather than to hard drugs. The person with a via lascivia would be very likely to consume endless cups of coffee or generous amounts of sugar on a daily basis. Compared with heroin or cocaine, these substances are relatively harmless, but are not all healthy, especially when consumed in excess. However, anyone with the via lascivia who takes hard drugs is almost certain to become addicted. A few may escape addiction because their bodies react so violently the first time they use drugs that they cannot try them a second time. Curiously, people with this marking are also prone to addiction to excitement, and are literally 'hooked' on the adrenalin rush their own body chemistry produces.

The straight form of the via lascivia has a milder meaning than the long, semi-circular form. The straight type can vary from a short dash to a long, deeply-etched marking. Small traces of this line occur in many hands, but a long, straight bar line is not at all common. The dramatic curving form that cuts the life line is also rare, occuring in fewer than one hand in a hundred.

This form of the via lascivia seems to indicate that the owner has a strong link to drugs in one form or another. It is astonishing how often those who have it become concerned with drugs. Some may suffer a medical problem which requires drugs for life, while others may work in the pharmaceutical industry as a researcher or pharmacist. In the days before heroin became widely used, palmists recorded a large proportion of chemists who had this marking. Nowadays, all kinds of people are involved in the production and distribution of illegal drugs, so one's neighbourhood chemist is not likely to have this line. The London Cheirological Society once found a nun with this mark and it turned out that her Order placed her in charge of the convent's medicine cabinet.

Why do so many naturopaths and other natural healers have the via lascivia in their hands? It is probably because these people discovered early in life that their bodies react badly to drugs and other chemicals. Childhood medicines may have made them seriously ill, and they turned away from conventional medicine and sought help from herbal remedies, acupuncture, and other drug free therapies. Inevitably, some of these people take up naturopathy as a career.

Some palmists have noted that occasionally natural healers have a faint yellow or orange tinge to the skin of their palms. This is not a sign of jaundice, but an indication that the person is probably a vegetarian whose diet is very high in carrots, pumpkin, and other sources of beta-carotene.

In addition, naturopaths tend to have the bottom phalanges of their fingers 'pinched-in' and rather thin, which is a sign of abstinence and self-discipline. It is the exact opposite of the thick, fleshy lower phalanges that indicate a self-indulgent personality, particularly in regard to food. We do know of a few solidly-built naturopathic doctors, but the majority are not big eaters and tend to be slender.

The hand seen in Figure 12.7 belongs to a woman naturopath of very high standing in her community. The medical stigmata can be seen very clearly in her hand below the somewhat deformed Mercury finger. Although she does not have the via lascivia, there is a distinct whorl on the mount of Luna, providing emphasis on intuitive faculties. She is a notably intuitive person, as her fingertips suggest. The basal phalanges of her fingers are not pinched-in, but are certainly thinner than the other two sections.

The hands of a chiropractor are similar to those of most natural healers, except that there are usually signs of strength in the hands. The fingertips may be slightly spatulate, the mount

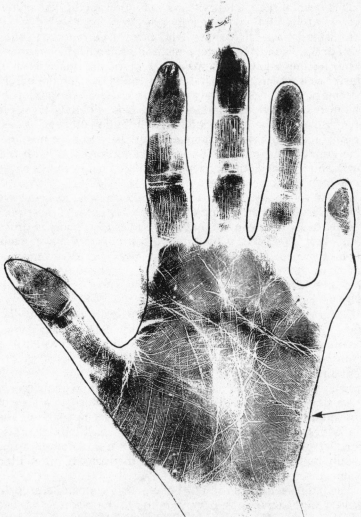

Figure 12.7: Hand print showing distinct whorl on the mount of Luna.

of Venus may be larger than normal, and the line of life will usually swing out into the palm in a nice curve.

Good massage therapists also tend to have strong hands, which are often also distinctly broad. The mount of Luna swells out in much the same way as it does on a sailor, and the mount of Venus is usually very large, giving the palm a roundish appearance.

An interesting illustration of a massage therapist's hand is

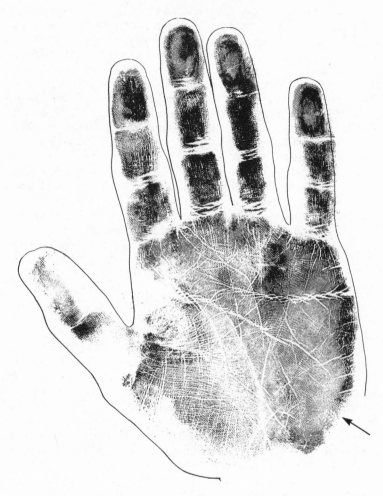

Figure 12.8: Hand print showing a distinct pattern on the lunar mount.

shown in Figure 12.8. While containing a number of the healer's traits described in this chapter (including the medical stigmata, and the long Apollo and Mercury fingers) this person's hand is typical of a person involved in massage. In addition to its general strength and breadth, the clear pattern on the lunar mount reveals a powerful instinctual current, which plays a major role in his work. In addition to maintaining a practice devoted to people (especially patients suffering from severe illnesses who are under a doctor's care), he is also one of a handful of massage therapists in the United States who perform therapeutic massage on show and race horses.

We need to make a clear distinction between the hands of people who dabble in massage as a hobby and those who have a genuine talent for this type of work. A great many people take up massage and are never more than adequate, while only a small percentage clearly possess a natural ability. Invariably they have the hands we have just described, whether they are female or male. It is interesting to note that men with hands like this tend to take up the sport of wrestling at some time in their lives, like the massage therapist described above. Needless to say, this is not yet true with women!

From natural healers we can turn to the hands of those who practise psychic or spiritual healing. We have no doubt that there are people who genuinely possess a healing gift. While some healers believe that they are simply a channel for the healing power of God, others believe that the gift is related to some special energy within themselves which they can transfer to others. Some who practise as professional healers simply achieve their results through the power of suggestion (as is the case with faith healing) and the soothing effect of their ministrations. This does not in any way diminish the importance of what they are doing. Old-fashioned tender loving care may be just what a sick body requires and may indeed speed up a sick person's rate of recovery. A strong dose of faith can work miracles too. The fact that no special ability on the healer's part is involved has no bearing if the patient gets well. However, if there is no special ability, you cannot expect to find anything in the hands.

Conversely, the few people who have the ability to heal (especially through what is known as 'magnetic healing') tend to share similar traits. In our experience, these people are solidly built and have strong earth hands. These hands may have a somewhat rough appearance, including coarse lines and skin texture. The hands also reveal a strong energy level and a large mount of Venus, an indication of a powerful sex drive.

By contrast, the minority of healers who believe that their healing power comes from a higher source tend to have hands that are thin, sensitive and 'spiritual-looking'. True psychic or spiritual healers often have fine vertical lines running up the inside of their fingers. These lines cluster thickly on the two lower phalanges and somewhat more thinly on the uppermost phalange. They are called *energy lines* in palmistry, and reveal that the person is pouring out energy in some way. The most common example is the person who is overworked and always tired. This person is like a leaky battery, and their own vital energy is being lost. They often need to relax and do something to recharge themselves, such as bathing in the sea or sitting quietly under some trees. Special exercises may help as well*. Psychic healers often have these marks not because they are necessarily tired, but because they are continually giving energy to others.

Bear in mind that the vast majority of people with the narrow hands described here do not have much, if any, healing ability. Remember too that most healers, however sincere, are not really doing anything that can be classified as 'psychic'.

Finally, it is important to remember that just because you lack certain healing aspects in your hands you should not avoid working in a helping profession. Before he began to study massage therapy, for example, the person whose hand is shown in Figure 12.8 had no samaritan lines whatsoever. Because palmistry reveals tendencies, the lines in the hand are subject to change, and are related both to outer circumstances and what we choose to do with our basic abilities.

*For further discussion, consult *Power Spots* by José A. Rosa, M.D. with Nathaniel Altman (The Aquarian Press, Wellingborough, 1986).

Chapter 13

OTHER HANDS

As we have seen from the previous chapters, many careers are related to specific hand traits. Most of these jobs can be grouped together, but there are others which do not fit conveniently into the previous chapters. We shall cover these careers in this chapter on 'other' hands.

Higher income careers in medicine and science are described in Chapters 11 and 12. The practice of law, which is often considered a prestigious career, attracts some very interesting hand types. Indeed, we could say that plain, ordinary hands are rarely found among members of the legal profession. The lines of the hands tend to be long and strong, the hand is either plump or muscular, and the fingerprint patterns nearly always noteworthy. There are few specific rules to follow regarding legal hands, but two lines occur regularly: the ring of Solomon and the fork at the end of the head line. The ring of Solomon was described in Chapter 11 and is a sign of psychological insight. The fork in the head line was described previously as the 'writer's fork'. Yet it is something more than that.

On occasion, a head line splits into two main branches halfway down its length. This should not be counted as a fork, because the true fork always consists of a short branching just at the end of the head line. It can occur on any type of head line but is most common among those which are fairly long. People with this mark have the ability to look at all sides of a question. They can consider more than one point of view. It is an invaluable gift in a writer, and is also found with marked frequency in legal hands.

Nearly all lawyers have prominent Mercury fingers. Sometimes the digit is long and strong, and often will be curved or at least somewhat irregular in shape. This reveals an astute, calculating turn of mind. When there is a distinct bend to this finger, there will be a devious side to the personality and the knack of turning situations to one's personal advantage. Marked straightness in the little finger is more likely to indicate scrupulous honesty. Judges (except those who previously worked as lawyers) nearly always tend to have this straight, long Mercury finger along with a powerful thumb and other typical features of the legal hand.

The print shown in Figure 13.1 is of a successful forty-year-old lawyer working in South America. Note the clear fork on his head line and the slight curve all the way along his Mercury finger. Although his hand does not possess a perfect ring of Solomon, he does have several fragments of a similar type on his mount of Jupiter. There is also a very strong line somewhat further down, curving from the mount of Saturn towards the start of the life line. The heart line reveals humanitarian tenden-

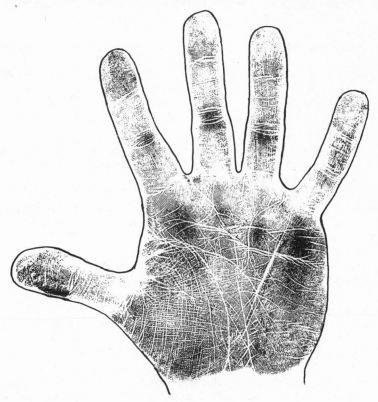

Figure 13.1: Hand print of a successful lawyer.

cies, and the strong loop of humour indicates a happy, optimistic nature.

A square tip on the thumb is not often found on legal hands but when it exists, it reveals a love of justice and fair play. People with this formation become upset when they encounter corruption or dishonesty and they set out to rectify it. People with square-tipped thumbs become excellent judges, whether sitting on the bench of the highest court in the land, or judging a local beauty contest or dog show. You can be sure that their judgement will not be swayed by personal preference. We have to admit that this trait is seldom found among members of the legal fraternity. We've seen it a few times with solicitors who work with minority groups and for social causes. In actual fact, the square-tipped thumb is most commonly found among skilled mechanics. Nevertheless, this feature still indicates a love of justice.

In Chapter 10 we wrote that square fingertips are often associated with accountants and mathematicians. People with squarish tips love an ordered and structured style of work. However there are two more fields which attract people with square fingertips: the armed forces and the police. We must admit that this feature is more commonly found among men than women, because females who enlist in the armed forces tend to be more individualistic and may have almost any type of hand. Female hands in these fields are often strong and sturdy, but there are enough exceptions to prevent our theory on square tips from becoming a rule.

There is a difference between the military hands found during peacetime and those of soldiers going to war. In times of war, men of all types either enlist or get drafted. During times of peace, mainly squared-tipped men join the military, particularly those who want to make it a career. Military life is totally ordered. There is a time to wake up, a time to go to bed, and a way to cut your hair, tie your shoelaces and lay out your belongings. Who but a square fingertipped man could enjoy this? An army saying teaches that 'There are three ways to do anything — the right way, the wrong way, and the army way'. The army way may be cumbersome and inflexible, but it is always very effective.

Military hands tend to be strong and masculine as well as square-tipped. Loops will be more common than any other fingerprint pattern, though the proportion of other types will rise among the officers. At the very bottom of the military hierarchy, among those who will never get beyond 'footslogger duties' will be people with a high incidence of defective head lines and other poor features in the hand.

Law enforcement also attracts people with square-tipped fingers, and there is no obvious way to distinguish them from members of other square-tipped professions except that their hands tend to be strong and masculine like those who are attracted to a military career. However, one subtle clue lies in the skin texture of the back of the hand. Military hands often have a slight grainy texture to them. This can also be seen in the hands of garage mechanics even after a careful scrubbing with soap and water. The skin texture seems to be associated with the use of machinery and is never found on office workers. The hands of police officers do not appear to have it either, although we have encountered many policemen who had previously served in the armed forces.

Another interesting feature we sometimes encounter in law enforcement and the military is a well-developed mount of Mars. The mount is located in the area below where the life line begins, just above the top of the mount of Venus. Most people have no distinct pad here and the area is simply a web of skin. A few people have a developed mount which betrays a courageous personality. Those who have it never back away from conflict, and are always ready to fight for a worthy cause. Firemen, police officers and others who exhibit conspicuous bravery tend to have this trait, as do boxers and those proficient in the martial arts. This does not mean that the person is aggressive in the sense of being a trouble-maker. Rather, a strong mount of Mars is the sign of a crusader and a warrior. It is at least as common among women as men.

Soldiers with this mount are usually men who volunteered for service as soon as they were old enough to do so. They dream of warfare when young and hope to go into active service as soon as possible. A soldier with this feature but with no prospects of going into battle may take up boxing or target practice in his spare time. In his personal life, he is inclined to challenge others. He is not actively seeking trouble or conflict, but is merely letting everyone know that he will stand up for what he believes in. Of course, in these cases it is important to examine the entire hand for aspects which will either strengthen or modify this somewhat annoying personality trait.

A family may pass the developed mount of Mars down through several generations. It will often be found on people who can claim ancestors who were prominent in the military. Naval personnel commonly have the typical 'sailor's patterns' discussed in Chapter 5. Air Force pilots, however, are not known to have special patterns in their hands.

Thirty years ago, both civilian and military pilots did share one common feature, even though it could not be used solely to identify their profession. Their index fingers were invariably straight and well-formed. Such well-shaped fingers usually accompany perfect eyesight, for reasons discussed below. Nowadays, perfect vision is not a prerequisite for flying, so this rule no longer holds. Nevertheless, we have found that straight Jupiter fingers are still common among both amateur and professional pilots.

The connection between eyesight and a straight Jupiter finger was first noted by the eccentric German palmist, Julius Spier. He was the originator of many theories which have not proved true, though a few others have been found to be strikingly accurate. A cursory examination of hands reveals that people with curved index fingers usually wear glasses, while those with straight Jupiter fingers rarely do.

Certain professions appear to attract people with good eyesight. Driving is one of them. Truck drivers and long distance coach drivers are, on the whole, spectacle free. Pilots – particularly in the Air Force – are still inclined to have perfect vision and straight index fingers. Professional athletes often conform to this pattern as well.

The theory behind this curious link between the hands and the eyes lies in the connection between eyesight and personality. There is mounting evidence that myopia and astigmatism are not simply the result of genetics, but can be linked to definite personality traits. This theory was introduced by the ophthalmologist W.H. Bates in his book *Better Sight Without Glasses*, first published in 1920. Dr. Bates found that in the majority of individuals, myopia and astigmatism develop at around fourteen years of age, at the time when self-doubt and insecurity most often blossom as well. Spier believed that these traits are in turn reflected in the index finger, the symbol of Self. Whether the defective vision causes the weakness in the personality or vice versa, there is mounting evidence that they are indeed linked, and that the finger shapes correspond as well.

For a typical example of a pilot's hand, see Figure 13.2. The subject was a pilot in his twenties, and is presently a Senior Flight Engineer for a major airline. Notice his straight Jupiter finger and the way it seems to rise from the uppermost part of the palm. He has a clear, straight head line (suggesting realism) and a well-marked loop of seriousness. The fingers are somewhat knotted as well.

Airline flight attendants are also inclined to have long and well-formed Jupiter fingers. In addition to being innately ambitious, their jobs demand good organizing skills, and they need to be counted upon for clear thinking and leadership in an emergency. The long index finger is a symbol of self-assurance

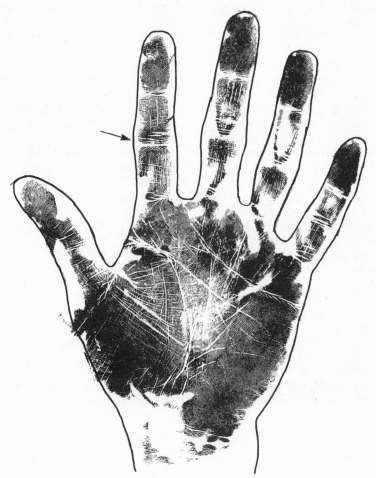

Figure 13.2: Hand print showing long straight Jupiter finger of an airline pilot.

and self-awareness, and reveals that its owner has the capacity to make the most of himself or herself in every possible way.

Because they do not work the traditional five-day week, many flight attendants pursue other interests, such as a part-time career in business or modelling. While many female flight attendants possess the long-fingered feminine hands of a model or an actress, others appear to have good business hands. In such cases, they often use their airline experience as a stepping-stone towards a career in business or in the hotel industry. We have also noted many hands with samaritan lines (an indication of healing ability) and loop fingerprint patterns, which reveal an innate ability to get on well with people and conform to an established routine.

Since flight attendants work in the public eye, they often have fate lines which rise from the mount of Luna. Ancient tradition links this mount to travel, and we have seen how often sailors have this mount well-developed. It is also interesting to note that people whose work involves flying great distances often have the fate line rising from the Luna mount. Public figures who have this line also tend to do a great deal of travelling.

While most life lines curve around the base of the thumb, people who travel a great deal often have a life line which ends on or near the mount of Luna. Traditionally, this indicates migration, and people who travel continually often have this line formation as well. In some cases an alternative feature appears that consists of two or three strong lines running to Luna from the life line as it approaches the bottom of the palm. For a good example of this marking, see Figure 9.3.

Another interesting pattern consists of dozens of short lines leaving the life line all along its length pointing in the general direction of Luna. These are the 'travel lines' which a palmist considers when reading events from the life line. Each line represents a journey. When a great number are found, you can be sure that you are dealing with someone who loves to travel, or travels for a living, as in the case of a pilot or flight attendant. They are illustrated in Figure 13.3.

Some palmists believe that travel lines can also be read from the side of the palm, as small horizontal lines moving up along the mount of Luna. Each line represents a major journey. The

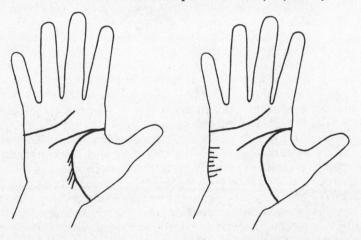

Figure 13.3: Travel lines.   *Figure 13.4:* Travel lines.

later in life travel occurs, the higher it will be found along the side of the hand (Figure 13.4).

Surprisingly, wealthy people who can afford to travel for pleasure whenever they wish rarely show a travel line for every trip. Only the first few journeys – or those of special importance – will be marked. For people such as this, it is possible that travel means little to them and therefore does not register in the hand. The hand of a person who makes five trips abroad per year is unlikely to reveal five separate lines for these trips, but a farmer who makes his first journey to a big city, even if it's only 300 miles from the farm, will probably have a strong travel line on his hand for this trip.

For a contrast to these types of 'travelling hands', observe the hands of a person with a very steady, quiet and undemanding job. The chances are that the life line will be completely bare. There are not many people like this, but the custodian, cloakroom attendant or lift-operator may well show this pattern. This would be especially true if they work for a large company and have security of tenure for their entire working life.

Those individuals providing public service such as waiters, waitresses, cashiers and shop assistants require the ability to get on well with others, and loop fingerprints are a great advantage. Among those working with the public, the thumb can be of any shape except blunt and heavy, for this will reveal a tendency to lack tact, diplomacy, and the ability to accommodate another point of view.

Many waiters and waitresses have fate lines starting from the mount of Luna, for they are certainly in the public eye. However, you would not be likely to find many with strong index fingers or signs of major talent, unless they are waiting at tables while pursuing another career like acting or writing, as many do. Some waiters may have the 'angles' of the thumb developed like those of a musician, as discussed in Chapter 9. These people require a sense of balance and smooth movement to get them around a crowded restaurant with heavily laden trays. There is a theory that people with 'sensitivity bumps' on their fingers (a sign of artistic creativity discussed in Chapter 7) never drop things. It would be interesting to see if the best tray-balancers have these bumps on their fingertips. Certainly many people who wait at tables have some degree of musical ability, and quite a few have worked as actors, dancers and singers.

Professional chefs have no specific features in their hands that point to their specific profession, but their hands are inclined to be fleshy (even hands of those who are not fat from overeating). We have yet to observe a thin or bony hand on anyone specializing in food preparation as a career. Among chefs, the bottom phalanges of the fingers deserve special attention. Broad, plump lower phalanges indicate self-indulgence and a love for sensate pleasures, such as eating. However, if the flesh of this phalange is not broad but instead forms a high pad that is not particularly wide, the owner has a well-developed sense of taste. Professional wine-tasters often have this formation, and it can occasionally be found on the finest chefs as well. The traditional fleshiness often found in the hands of chefs usually includes a full mount of Venus accompanied by a well-curved life line. The print shown in Figure 13.5 belongs to a successful thirty-seven-year-old chef and restaurateur. It exhibits the features described above perfectly. His arch fingerprints are of special interest, revealing his love of hard work and a good ability to create with

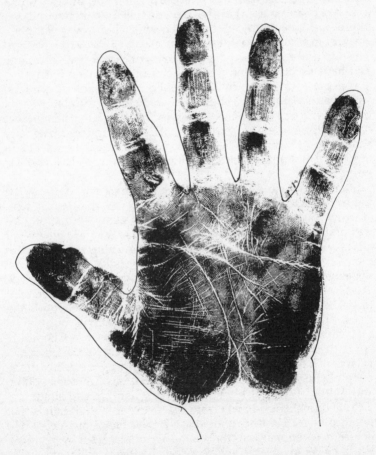

Figure 13.5: Hand print of a chef showing interesting arch fingerprints.

his hands. His strong nurturing qualities can be seen by the samaritan lines on the mount of Mercury.

Turning now from the hands of those who work with people, let's look at the hands of those who work with animals. There are a few markings which are often associated with work of this type, and the veterinary surgeon, the animal trainer, the jockey and the breeder of all varieties of beasts may well possess these marks in their hands.

The most common indication of work with animals is an almost microscopic pattern in the skin ridges of the palm. It is found among the apexes (or tri-radii) which are located under the fingers on top of the mounts. Most apexes are of the type shown in Figure 13.6a. Some people have the apex under the ring finger in the manner shown in Figure 13.6b, which is known as the 'animal affinity mark'. When found in one hand only, it simply indicates a love of animals. If present in both hands, the owner is apt to choose a career that is somehow involved with animals.

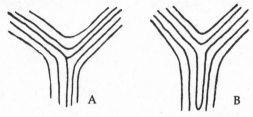

Figure 13.6: Normal tri-radius (A) and 'animal affinity' tri-radius (B).

Beryl Hutchinson, the former President of Britain's prestigious Society for the Study of Physiological Patterns (SSPP) reported that horse lovers frequently have a cross on the side of the Saturn finger, just below the nail. She found that many exhibitors at dog shows had several small crosses in this position as well.

Towards the beginning of this century, the redoubtable Mrs Robinson (author of the classic palmistry text *The Graven Palm*) also identified a 'horse' feature. She found that horse trainers and jockeys often had stars on the back of their fingers, particularly near the top and on the knuckles of the Saturn finger. In her day the horse was still a major means of transportation. We have seldom come across this marking nowadays, but the few examples we have seen appeared on the hands of those who were devoted horseback riders. We have also seen a few country people who work with animals frequently, and the top joints of their fingers were notably short. However, even though the marks described in these paragraphs are reliable indicators of working with animals, there are many people who work with animals who have none of these signs in their hands.

To complete our account of hands and careers, we thought we would comment on the hands of professional palmists. Palmistry is a psychological tool and most hand readers emphasize advice and counselling in their readings. As one would expect, the typical palmist has hands which resemble those of the social worker or psychologist. In addition, they often have the curved index finger described in Chapter 2. This pattern is frequently associated with people whose career is also a personal hobby, as is the case with most professional hand analysts.

There is also a specific trademark that is often found in the hands of palmists. It is an equilateral triangle which is formed by the health, fate and head lines, as illustrated in Figure 13.7. Like all special signs, it must be very clear and perfectly formed in order to be considered worthy of notice. First described in 1886 by Eveline Farwell in her book *Fingers and Fortune*, she called it 'the palmist's triangle', and it is as valid today as when she first identified it.

Figure 13.7: The palmist's triangle.

This mark is also found in the hand of astrologers, and we have a large number of prints of prominent astrologers and palmists who possess this otherwise uncommon sign. Over sixty per cent of palmists and astrologers have this mark, while perhaps less than ten per cent of the general public do. In Chapter 10 we pointed out that triangles are associated with technical skills of all types. The palmist's triangle is simply a specific case of this general principle. However, just because this triangle may not appear in your hands, you should not believe that you cannot become a competent (or even outstanding) hand analyst or astrologer!

Many people believe that all palm readers are clairvoyant or that they possess some special type of psychic skill. This legend has gained credence because many gypsy fortune-tellers claim to practise palmistry. In fact, hand analysis is a science and has no connection whatsoever with psychic powers. Sound knowledge, a compassionate heart and a good mind are the major requirements necessary to become a competent hand reader. The gypsies have no tradition of actually studying the hand, and merely use palmistry as an excuse to ply their dubious trade of telling fortunes.

That there are such things as psychic powers can hardly be denied. Most people have had at least one or two psychic experiences at some time in their lives and many have had traces of such faculties operating more or less continually. Unfortunately, genuine psychic ability can often be imitated through trickery, and large numbers of so-called psychic readers are no more than con artists. Those who do possess extra-sensory perception reveal this clearly in their hands. One glance at the hands of a genuine psychic can reveal whether there is any real ability or not.

The most striking sign of psychic ability is a pointed index finger. Most of us have this finger somewhat rounded. If it is definitely pointed, it is an indicator of a good deal of psychic awareness and often mystical qualities as well. The pointedness is usually more marked in the passive hand than the active hand, but if either Jupiter finger is pointed, the other is bound to be to some extent also. Old palmistry books associated these fingers with spiritualism, but somehow this interpretation has not been carried forward into modern books. This may be due to the fact that spiritualism is not as common today as it was in the past. It is also probable that years ago the term 'spiritualism' meant what we now call 'psychic'. At the present time, the spiritualist movement is only a small part of the whole metaphysical field. However, we still find pointed index fingers among the world's top spiritualist mediums as well as psychics who work with cards or crystal balls.

Next in importance when determining psychic ability in the hand are the dermatoglyphic patterns. The most common is a loop on the mount of Luna. Among the good psychics we have known, at least half of them have this pattern. Anyone with this loop will be prone to sensing things about other people. They often have a telepathic link with other family members. A woman with this mark will be liable to say that 'I always know when my daughter will ring me or when a friend or relative is in trouble'. From being able to 'tune in' to family and friends to offering psychic readings to the public is not a big step. Such a person often tends to dabble in reading tarot or playing cards

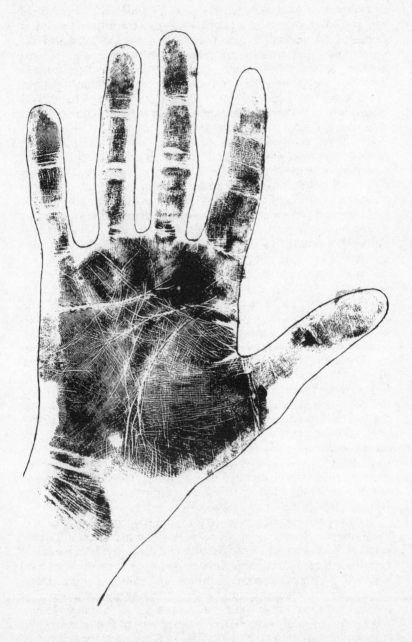

Figure 13.8: Hand print showing pointed Jupiter finger and the 'psychic' loop on the mount of Luna.

and discovers that they seem to 'work' in a miraculous fashion.

If you have this loop in your hands, you may want to explore this field more deeply. We mentioned earlier that this loop is often found on a swollen mount of Luna in the hands of many sailors. Tradition states that sailors are superstitious, but the truth is that they are often more psychic than their land-dwelling friends.

The hand shown in Figure 13.8 belongs to the famous medium Bill Rowan, who has demonstrated his psychic ability before scientists in Europe, Australia and Japan. Born in Scotland, Bill has packed halls across the British Isles with his lectures and displays of mediumship. His hand clearly reveals both the pointed Jupiter finger and the 'psychic' loop in the mount of

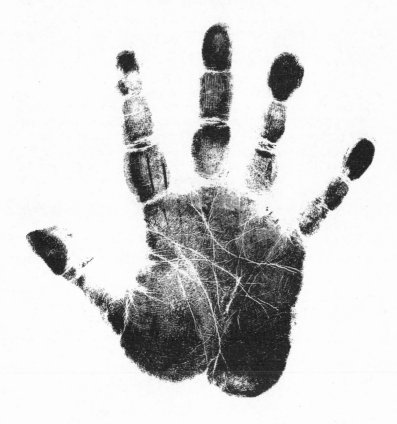

Figure 13.9: Hand print showing a rare 'line of clairvoyance'.

Luna. The two Apollo lines from the side of the palm are also noteworthy.

Fingerprints may also offer some clues to psychic ability. If the ring finger and little finger both have whorl prints – with an absence of whorls on the other fingers – the owner of the hand will be prone to experiencing precognitive dreams. This is simply extra-sensory perception operating from below the conscious level. Anyone who experiences this may also be inclined to receive impressions in their waking state in the forms of hunches or premonitions. It is also possible to bring unconscious ESP up to the conscious level with the aid of simple tools like a divining rod or pendulum.

Any type of dermatoglyphic patterns on the mount of Luna will emphasize the creative or intuitive powers in some manner or other. Whorls on Luna reveal the ability to visualize strongly. Any other type of pattern may suggest some kind of psychic talent.

Mediums in the spiritualist movement often have strong health (or Mercury) lines. This line is rather badly named because although it can indicate health problems, it also has much to reveal about the subconscious mind. If you find such a line on a professional psychic, it would strongly indicate that he or she possesses genuine ability. Occasionally, the health line is formed in a graceful bow shaped curve, as shown in Figure 13.9. This is traditionally known as the 'line of clairvoyance', but it is very rare. It appears to relate more to spiritual gifts than to psychic ability alone.

PART III: *PRACTICAL PALMISTRY*

Chapter 14

PALMISTRY AND CAREER COUNSELLING

For the serious hand analyst, providing career guidance through the careful examination and interpretation of the form and markings of the hand is both a privilege and a responsibility. For this reason, we need to seek a balance between a caring, compassionate attitude and the desire to maintain high standards of accuracy and thoroughness when a person seeks our help. Although our primary task is to provide both general and specific information about the individual's character, career possibilities and life path, we must at the same time avoid trying to control the person's life. We need to recognize the areas of both talent and difficulty which we see in the hand, while offering clarity and support in the individual's choice of career direction and movement.

Special consideration needs to be given to the younger person. Generally, we are opposed in principle to advising preteens about specific career directions. The hands of children are especially prone to change, and any coercion (whether subtle or not) by adults can have a negative effect on both the child's personality and career satisfaction in the long run. Of course, if a child shows a special aptitude or interest in a particular area, there should be no reason why he or she cannot receive parental encouragement or support.

In the majority of cases, we feel that the most beneficial time for a career-oriented hand analysis is between the ages of fifteen and eighteen, when the young person is beginning to seriously consider future career plans. When we examine the hands of a younger person, we should not immediately focus on specifics, but should attempt to get a bearing on the person's *general direction*, taking both personal interests and aptitudes into account.

Is this person extroverted or introverted? Is he or she 'people oriented' or does he or she prefer to work alone? Is his or her hand more the type that enjoys physical activity, or is he or she more suited for intellectual work? By determining the type of hand the person has, along with its flexibility, shape of thumb, dominant fingerprint patterns, and finger formation and place-ment, we can gather an abundance of useful data. This in turn will give us a good overview of the subject's personality and life direction. From this general understanding, we can proceed towards a more profound and specific analysis of the hands.

The more specific phase of the analysis may be a good oppor-tunity for the recipient of the reading to ask questions, so that they will take a more active role in the reading rather than re-main a passive listener. This participation also leads to their seeking solutions to questions and problems themselves. Very often human beings know the solution to their problems on a deeper level, but are accustomed to avoiding them or having so-meone else provide the answers. A hand analysis can help the person to bring these answers to the surface.

In some cases, the fate line will be tied to the line of life, in-dicating that the parents are exerting a strong influence on the subject's career direction. This may be either real or imagined, reflected by the statement, 'What will others think of me?' This configuration is often accompanied by tied life and head lines.

In other cases, the fate line will begin at a point on the palm that indicates being grounded in a satisfying career at a later time in life, indicating that the individual will be a 'late bloomer'. Because there should be no set timetable for when someone's career should begin, such information is important to share. Because the lines of the hand are subject to change, revealing these trends with the client can help him or her to make clear decisions based on genuine needs and aspirations rather than on what society expects of them at the time.

On occasion we have analysed hands which revealed no specific career direction at all, indicating that their owners were suited for no particular line of work. This often occurs with peo-ple who have never had any idea what they have wanted to do in life. In such cases, it is useful to suggest one or two career directions that are within the range of the individual's talent. If appropriate, encourage the client to stick to their chosen field rather than jump from one job to another.

There are also times when you will be asked to read the hands of people in their early to mid-twenties who have never worked at all. They often end up living on the street, engaging in petty crime or becoming dependent on public assistance for life. In these cases, hand analysis can often identify the deeper psychological currents which helped to create the situation. While the palmist's role is not that of therapist, sharing information related to underlying personality issues can be very useful to the person seeking a consultation, as it helps them to gain a deeper, more objective understanding of their situation. As a general rule, we encourage such people to break out of their stagnant pattern and establish momentum by performing odd jobs, working at a flea market or on a farm, or finding some other kind of legal temporary work. In addition to gaining valuable experience, opportunities for more fulfilling and stable employment may present themselves.

In past generations, the traditional career direction was to adopt a single profession for one's entire working life. However, there is a trend today towards devoting oneself to two or even three part-time careers at the same time. In our own cases, we balance careers as writers (on a variety of subjects), lecturers and professional palmists. As people continue to expand their personal interests, the trend towards career diversification will more and more become accepted as the norm.

Finally, we need to also bear in mind that a career has different meanings to different people. For some, their profession may be an overriding passion in life. It may play a central role in almost everything they do, and be a major focus for their time, talent and energy. For others, their career will exist primarily to earn money in order to support outside interests. We know of more than one businessperson whose career supports a love for travel. Painting, writing, and involvement in political activity are just a few of many areas of deep personal interest which are subsidized by primarily 'money-making' careers that are of secondary value to the worker.

The midlife crisis is of special interest to the hand analyst. The vast majority, if not all, of the people we read for experience this period during their lives, which often manifests as problems with work. The midlife crisis may bring about the need to make minor adjustments in career patterns and direction, or may cause a traumatic break with the past and a profound re-evaluation of one's life and its purpose.

In many hands, the midlife crisis can be seen by the ending of the Saturn or fate line and the appearance of another (and often overlapping) fate line. This will indicate a relatively easy shift into a new line of work at the age the line reflects. In some cases, a second career is indicated as a strong parallel line to the line of fate. In others, the original fate line ends at between forty and forty-five years of age, indicating a period of drift and unhappiness in one's career. This may, however, be followed by another fate line further up on the palm, revealing that after several years of uncertainty or dissatisfaction, a new career path begins.

This feature is often accompanied by an obvious bending of the Saturn and Apollo fingers towards each other, indicating general frustration with one's life path and the feeling of being trapped. However, this configuration may be ameliorated by the presence of a clear and prominent line of Apollo (or Sun line) which reveals the capacity to cope with changes in one's career.

Although difficult signs to have in the hand, the crisis they reflect can – if properly worked with – open the door to new career interests and a deeper level of self-understanding. Rather than being seen as negative, a problem revealed by something like a broken fate line can signal the beginning of an exciting process of personal growth.

It is important to remember that for some, the work cycle need not extend to the traditional age of sixty-five or seventy. Our society glorifies people (especially men) who cling relentlessly to a career until they are forced to retire, especially if they accumulate vast sums of money in the process. Very often, they never live long enough to enjoy this money, which is usually shared by the tax people and surviving relatives. During their middle years, men often lose their original interest in their careers, but continue working even if they don't need the money. They are either using work to avoid being with their wives, are afraid of the freedom that their new life would bring, or simply want to maintain the image as a responsible worker and provider.

For others – especially those who have prominent fate lines which reach the top of the hand or even penetrate the Saturn finger – retirement at any age may not even be a viable option at all. One of the beauties of palmistry is that it objectively reflects the needs and abilities of each individual. Rather than encourage the person to fit into whatever patterns society deems acceptable, it provides a perspective through which we can evaluate our own needs without coercion or pre-judgement.

For many individuals, and men in particular, the ending of their working lives brings about a major life crisis. However, rather than being seen as a time of boredom, inactivity, declining health and loneliness, the later years can also be a time for utilizing one's maturity and life experience to create new opportunities for learning, pleasure, discovery and service.

There are no special signs in the hand that can offer guidance to potential retirees. However, we have found that those with a good Apollo line are better able to cope with life changes. People with a clear and long Apollo line are more prone to make an easy transition from a work routine to a life involving more personal choices.

For many who approach retirement age, the best help a hand reader can provide is to encourage the person to take stock of their life and to explore their major interests apart from work. Being free of the traditional work patterns offers time for reading, travel, painting the house, working as a volunteer, serving as a mentor to a younger person, gardening, athletics, pursuing a hobby or craft, writing, fishing, dreaming, socializing, or simply doing nothing at all.

When practised with care, sensitivity and humility, hand analysis can be a valuable tool for helping people discover their true task in life. By helping others better understand their talents, abilities and areas of difficulty, we help them to achieve their fullest potential as human beings.

Chapter 15

HOW TO TAKE HAND PRINTS

One of the best ways to deepen our understanding of the hand is to have a record of the hands we analyse. The easiest and most economical method for recording hands is the taking of hand prints. Although the prints do not always reveal the many dimensions of the human hand, the shape, lines and skin ridge patterns (dermatoglyphics) can, with practice, be faithfully reproduced. When used in conjunction with the Hand Analysis Test Chart described on page 201, a collection of hand prints can be very useful for both the palmist and the people whose hands he or she analyses. In addition to providing a permanent record of the hand itself, we have found that subsequent follow-up prints can reveal changes in the hands over the years.

Materials
The materials necessary for taking hand prints are both inexpensive and relatively easy to obtain. To take a hand print you will require the following:

1. A rubber roller approximately 4 inches (10 cm) wide.
2. A tube of black water-based block printing (lino) ink. Rowney's (see page 204) is our favourite, but Speedball (available in the USA) is an acceptable alternative.
3. Good quality art paper. You may prefer single sheets or a spiral-bound art book for easier storage.
4. A thin pad of foam rubber to provide a suitable cushion for the paper.
5. A sheet of glass, linoleum or newspaper for applying the ink.

Procedure

1. First, lay the paper over the foam rubber, which helps mould the paper to conform to the contours of the hand. Roll out the ink on the glass, linoleum or newspaper (Figure 15.1).
2. Carefully ink the subject's hand, using just enough ink to lightly cover the entire palmar surface. You may want to cover part of the wrist as well (Figure 15.2).

Figure 15.1: Rolling out the ink.

Figure 15.2: Inking the hand.

3. Have the subject place their hand on the paper in a natural way, either from a sitting or standing position. Apply pressure to the entire hand (paying special attention to the centre of the palm and the space between the finger mounts) in order to obtain a complete impression (Figure 15.3). At this point you may also wish to make an outline of the hand

Figure 15.3: Placing the hand on the paper.

Figure 15.4: Holding the paper to prevent blurring.

with a pencil (or with a pen if you are confident of your drawing ability).

4. Hold the paper to the table as the hand is slowly withdrawn. This will prevent the print from blurring (Figure 15.4).

In addition to the print itself, we suggest that you include a record of the major features of the hand, such as the hand type, dominant fingers and mounts, fingerprint patterns, as well as personal data concerning the individual whose print you are including in your collection. A suggested Hand Analysis Test Chart follows for your convenience.

HAND ANALYSIS TEST CHART

Name:
Date of birth:
Today's date:

Predominant hand type:
Strongest mounts:
Weakest mounts:

Tests
Skin texture
Skin colour
Flexibility
Consistency

Fingers (describe, including fingerprint pattern)
Jupiter
Saturn
Apollo
Mercury
Predominant
Longer or shorter than palm
Straight
Bent

Thumb
Size
Flexibility
How set (low, medium, high)
Will phalange (describe)
Logic phalange (describe)

Nails
Size
Shape
Colour
Unusual features

Additional comments/personal data

ANNOTATED
BIBLIOGRAPHY

The Victorian period witnessed a great boom in palmistry. Three books stand out above all the others.

Benham, William G., *The Laws of Scientific Hand Reading* (New York: Putnam & Co., 1958).
Cheiro, *The Language of the Hand* (London: Herbert Jenkins, Ltd., 1980).
St. Hill, Katherine, *The Book of the Hand* (New Delhi: Sagar Publications, 1981).

The middle part of this century has given rise to the first 'twentieth-century style' of palmistry. The outstanding author of this era was Noel Jaquin. His best books include:

The Hand of Man (London: Faber and Faber, 1937).
The Signature of Time (London: Faber and Faber, 1950).
Man's Revealing Hands (London: Routledge & Kegan Paul, Ltd., 1934).

Several of his books have been republished in India.

A scientist working during the same period as Mr Jaquin was Dr. Charlotte Wolff. She wrote three books, two of which have been reprinted in India by Sagar Publications.

Studies in Hand Reading (London: Chatto & Windus, 1936).
The Human Hand (New York: Alfred A. Knopf, 1943).
The Hand in Psychological Diagnosis (London: Metheun, 1951).

The following books deal specifically with palmistry and vocational guidance:

Benham, William G., *How to Choose Vocations from the Hand* (New Delhi: Sagar Publications, 1968). This book is based on Benham's theory of mounts.

Brandon-Jones, David, *Your Hand and Your Career* (London: Arrow Books, 1980). The material presented in this book is based on the author's personal experience.

MacKenzie, Nancy, *Palmistry for Women* (New York: Warner Books, 1973). A good feminist book with prints of successful career women.

Meier, Nellie Simmons, *Lion's Paws* (New York: Barrows Mussey, 1937). This classic work contains hand prints of famous people from many walks of life.

Oxenford, Ina, *Modern Palmistry* (London: Bazaar Exchange & Mart, 1943). Contains an interesting chapter on careers.

Vartek, S.R., *Palmistry and Vocational Guidance* (New Delhi: Sagar Publications, 1964). This book is based largely on the teachings of Noel Jaquin.

Other palmistry books we have referred to in the text include:

Altman, Nathaniel, *The Palmistry Workbook* (Wellingborough: The Aquarian Press, 1984).

Farwell, Eveline, *Fingers & Fortune* (London, D. Scott, 1986).

Fitzherbert, Andrew, *Hand Psychology* (Sydney and London: Angus & Robertson, 1986).

Gettings, Fred, *The Book of the Hand* (London: Paul Hamlyn, 1965). This book is essential reading.

Hutchinson, Beryl B., *Your Life in Your Hands*, (London: Neville Spearman, 1967). This book is also essential reading.

Robinson, Mrs. A., *The Graven Palm* (London: Herbert Jenkins, Ltd., 1924). A rare classic.

Sen, K.C., *Hast Samudrika Shastra* (Bombay: D.B. Taraporevala, 1960).

Spier, Julius, *The Hands of Children* (London: Routledge & Kegan Paul, Ltd., 1955). Later reprinted in India.

The following publications dealing with careers provided additional source material for this book.

Bolles, Richard Nelson, *What Color is Your Parachute?* (Berkeley: Ten Speed Press, 1986).

Clarke, Roger, *Work in Crisis* (Edinburgh: St. Andrews Press, 1982).

De Board, Robert, *Counselling People at Work* (Aldershot, Hants: Gower Publishing Co. Ltd., 1983).

Elsberry, Richard B., 'Set Free', *The New York Times Magazine*, 4 January 1987, p. 37.

Mitchell, Joyce Slayton, *Choices and Changes* (New York: The College Board, 1982).

Occupational Projections and Training Data (Washington: Department of Labor, Bureau of Labor Statistics, 1980).

Paterson, T.T., *Job Evaluation*, vol.1 (London: Business Books, Ltd., 1972).

Schwartz, Lester, and Brechner, Irv, *Career Tracks* (New York: Ballantine Books, 1985).

Weinstein, Robert V., *Jobs for the 21st Century* (New York: Collier Books, 1983).

For information on the connection between eyesight and personality, the following books are recommended.

Bates, W.H., *Perfect Eyesight Without Glasses* (New York: Central Fixation Publications, 1920).

Corbett, Margaret, *Help Yourself to Better Sight* (North Hollywood: Wilshire Publishing Co., 1968).

Goodridge, Janet, *Natural Vision Improvement* (Richmond, Australia: Greenhouse Publications, 1985). A highly recommended modern volume.

Price, C.S., *The Improvement of Eyesight by Natural Methods* (London: Chapman & Hall, 1943). A highly regarded work by a medical doctor.

For serious American palmists, another good water-based ink for making hand prints is *Search* fingerprint slab ink. Direct enquiries to: Sirchie Finger Print Laboratories, PO Box 30576, Raleigh, North Carolina 27612 USA.

In England, The Reeves Shop, Kensington High Street, London, sells Reeves' own fingerprint ink. Modern block-printing inks and screen-printing inks are seldom suitable for fingerprintings. At one time, block-printing inks were made from organic materials and made good hand prints. Modern synthetic inks do not. The only one we can recommend is Rowney's Water Soluble Block Printing Colour, made by George Rowney and Co. Ltd of Bracknell, Berkshire, England.

Printers' Ink, of the type used to print newspapers, will also take good hand prints. It requires a good solvent to clean it off the hands afterwards.